Peace Like a River

Peace Like a River

Sallie Chesham

THE SALVATION ARMY SUPPLIES AND
PURCHASING DEPARTMENT
Atlanta, Georgia

The Author

Sallie Chesham is a Salvation Army Colonel, wife, mother of two grown children, author of a Salvation Army history, and three other recent books, *Walking With The Wind, Trouble Doesn't Happen Next Tuesday,* and *Today Is Yours.* At present, Sallie lives with her husband, Lt. Colonel Howard Chesham, in Boston where she serves on the staff of The Salvation Army's Harbor Light Center for Alcoholic Rehabilitation.

Copyright © 1981 by The Salvation Army
ISBN: 0-86544-014-X
Printed in the United States of America
First printing, May 1981
Second printing, December 1981
Third printing, February 1983

Contents

The following books by Samuel Logan Brengle are currently available through bookstores or Salvation Army Supplies and Purchasing Departments:

Heart Talks On Holiness
Resurrection Life and Power
The Soul Winner's Secret
The Way of Holiness
When The Holy Ghost Is Come
Love Slaves
Guest of the Soul
Helps to Holiness
Ancient Prophets (And Modern Problems)

Also available is *Portrait of a Prophet*, the life story of Samuel Logan Brengle, by Clarence W. Hall.

Preface

Peace Like a River is written out of compulsion. For a long time I've been interested, even eager to present certain aspects of truth as I perceive them, using as little religious jargon as possible, writing to the mind with a more secular though often simpler word choice. However, other writing kept waving for attention and I wrote on. Then, during the autumn of 1976, material came to my attention which would not be placated but seemed to keep shouting, "Now! Now!"

This is what happened: Brigadier Earl Lord of The Salvation Army, now retired, traveled extensively for some years as soloist and secretary with the famed holiness preacher and teacher, Commissioner Samuel Logan Brengle, with whom he shared intimate fellowship until Brengle's promotion to Glory on May 20, 1936. He preserved Brengle's personal letters to him, written over a period of 10 years. The friendship continued with Brengle's daughter, Elizabeth Brengle Reed.

Hearing of this association, Major Fred Ruth, principal of the Salvation Army School for Officers Training in Atlanta, Georgia, invited Lord to lecture his cadets. So much interest was expressed in the material's being put into print that Earl asked me to look over his letters and other memorabilia, including Brengle's Bible, newspaper clippings, and photographs. A contact was also made with Brengle's daughter Elizabeth and her son Logan, who shared recollections and prized writings, photographs and other treasures. So absorbed did I become that work was interrupted on another manuscript. "Now! Now!" I believe God ordered through the materials. Now, then, it is. I shall continually pray that many readers will gain as much from these newly discovered Brengle counsels as I have.

It seemed imperative that biographical sketches of Brengle, his adored wife Elizabeth, and the young Earl Lord be introduced preceding the letters, in order that the reader may be prepared for Brenglian insights, Scriptural choices and ruminations. *Peace Like a River*, then, is a look into the life and teaching of Samuel Logan Brengle; his wife, Elizabeth Swift Brengle; and their influence upon a very young, sometimes frustrated and tempted Captain in the ranks of The Salvation Army. The book leans heavily upon recollections of Elizabeth Reed and Earl Lord; Clarence Hall's biography, *Portrait of a Prophet;* Eileen Douglas' biography, *Elizabeth Swift Brengle;* writings of Samuel and Elizabeth Brengle; *Handbook of Doctrine* of The Salvation Army; and *Orders and Regulations for Field Officers* of The Salvation Army.

That the legendary Brengle was a flesh-and-blood man, prone to all the usual joys, sorrows, temptations, and disappointments of every man is attested in this record. It is also certified that wife Elizabeth was as important to the Brengle contribution as if she had physically shared both preaching and literary ministries. Their spiritual affinity was so choice that they cannot be said to have lived separated lives, though often thousands of miles apart, let alone have separate ministries.

Peace Like a River is a premise for your consideration, illustrated life-size by a man and woman who were young at the onset of this experience, intelligent, educated, proud, discerning, sensitive, and appealing. The woman had charm, wealth, culture, a curious mind, popularity; the man had been offered unusual opportunity for recognition, power and wealth, in a field not overcrowded with men of similar talent.

The importance of the Brengles flashes before me in exclamatory fashion as I recall the tragedy in the life of another idealistic, ambitious, talented young person, in many ways much like the young Brengles.

"I just can't take any more!" he shouted after months of self-torture in disillusionment with society and personal relationships. Then, among restraining friends, he grabbed a hidden gun, held it to his temple and committed suicide. He was not an alcoholic or drug addict; he had no money problems, and no need for recognition, for he enjoyed nation-wide popularity. He had always benefited from parental love and guidance and had a strong belief in God. In fact, he was a Christian. Yet sorrow, frustration, and disillusionment proved overwhelming.

Why?

That life itself seems unbearable, insane, often ladling out more distress than can be endured, is today acknowledged by leading professionals in every field, and is the anguished admission of the hurt in every age, group, and class. So many have lost faith in friends, the arts, business, professions, government, self—and God.

If, this moment, into *your* hand were placed a key with which you could immediately open a near door to a new life that would offer purpose, peace, a sense of acceptance of self and others, a guarantee of victory over temptation, assurance of joy in living, and belief that there is something even better coming after death, would you use it? A fringe benefit would be the fact that by so doing you could influence numbers of other folk toward victorious living.

Elizabeth, Earl, and I happily share what we believe to be new insights into two lives put wholly into God's keeping—one so luminous as to be termed saint by multitudes, the other so little known as often to be recognized only as "the wife" of the great Brengle. It is hoped that this Brenglian data will support the assertion that the key here described is the great reality for today and is both accessible to and practical for any sincere spiritual explorer.

Brengle suffered many of the same frustrations as did the youth who committed suicide but, discovering a key, not only proved strong enough to withstand intense and often sustained aggravation throughout a long life but also at its conclusion, though widowed, deaf, near-blind, and enduring a severely malfunctioning heart, died with a resounding "Hallellujah!" What is more astounding, identical results are guaranteed if the key is personally accepted and habitually used.

We invite you to observe Sam and Lily Brengle, and young Earl Lord, their lives, message, and methods, praying that not one reader will leave the place of the key despairing, "I just can't take any more!" but rather declaring, "I can take *anything* that comes!"

Marching on!

Sallie Chesham

One

Samuel Logan Brengle

Any man is captivating who holds in the pocket of his heart the key to inner peace; and if he should have both the desire and the ability to share that treasure with others, his life is worth examining. Samuel Logan Brengle is such a man. Acquiring the key in his twenties, he immediately began to attract and influence others, and so profound was that influence in later years that an extraordinary confusion took place. This illustration is typical of what happened:

In a western U.S.A. town he visited a businessman's home but spoke only to a small son. In the evening the man asked, "Were there any callers today?"

"Yes!" said the boy, "One."

"What was his name?"

"He didn't tell me, but I know who he is. His name is Jesus."

Samuel Logan Brengle is a legend in Salvation Army ranks and among many other cordons of spiritual adventurers. His name brings a sense of awe into conversation. After fifty years his books still leap sectarian hurdles and answer thousands of questions in many languages, including Braille; even his photograph appears to invigorate. Why? That is the reason for this inquiry and statement. Brengle's intense and trustful belief in God is, of course, the answer, but many people yearn for specifics. Many would like to know more about the man, aside from the pulpit and the preachment, and of the wife left home to rear his children during a lifetime of world-girdling, exhaustive journeys.

In lay language, some ask, tell how this relationship began. What technique or discipline was responsible for its growth? Did it bear him up through the trials other men endure? Was he, in fact, as other men—with similar physical, mental, and spiritual temptations, achievements, and defeats? Did he struggle for the wisdom he attained? Did he endure physical ailment and disability? What about loneliness? What about money and other possessions? What about anger, greed, lust, unbelief, depression? What about old age? What about death? How did he meet the death of his wife—and the specter of his own? Finally, how did he communicate his findings to others?

That he touched human experience broadly and deeply is established. At his funeral in May of 1936, it was stated that his loss to the international Salvation Army was inexpressible for he was a world-renowned "traveler, author, evangelist, counselor, teacher, student, fiery prophet, apostle, and friend." In his 49 years of Salvation Army officership he had seen more than 100,000 persons make decisions for God. Throughout his long life, he had traveled the North American continent many times, Australasia, the British Isles and Scandinavia. Many of his campaigns had brought long-lasting results. If this man Brengle can be proved to be flesh-and-blood, with an authentic and dependable experience of victorious living, then some today may listen to him. We'll properly then, though not too piously, begin at the beginning:

Five years before William Booth started The Salvation Army as a small preaching mission on London's lower east side, Samuel Logan Brengle was born in Fredericksburg, Indiana, on June 1,

1860, to William Nelson Brengle, schoolteacher, and Rebecca Horner Brengle. William Brengle, though a Presbyterian, had been elected superintendent of the Methodist Sunday school, finding no church of his chosen denomination nearby.

Baby Sam had been so named for his mother's brother who became a doctor because he "couldn't bear to see folks suffer" and "Logan" for his father's brother who'd changed church affiliation because he "felt led that way."

The marriage of Sam's parents in 1859 had been the social event of the year in the little town, which had both respect and devotion for the young schoolteacher, whose American heritage stretched back to 1762, when the first Brengle forebears settled in Maryland, then wheeled westward to Kentucky, 13 years before the Declaration of Independence.

Pioneers these, joining the land to make a living, and finding both friend and foe in Indians, animals, and other growing things. George D. Brengle, Sam's grandfather, worked as a blacksmith in Fredericksburg, Indiana, sired 11 children and saw that they all were educated as well as the backwoods schools could manage, urging them to hard work, independence, and high purpose. Two became preachers, James for 30 years pastor of a Presbyterian church in Croydon, Iowa, and Logan, in the United Brethren church. William Nelson, Sam's father, the most reserved member of the family, became a public schoolteacher.

In 1862, when Sam was two, his father left for the war between the states, helping an older man to recruit a company of volunteers. He was commissioned a first lieutenant, was captured, and escaped. His bravery and disciplinarianism were noted by many home-coming soldiers. He returned home an invalid, wounded during the siege of Vicksburg, and soon died, leaving a stunned young wife and a baby. All Sam later remembered of his father was his mother telling him between sobs, "Papa has gone to be with God." For some time, he tended to hyphen the two:

God-death; death-God, as if they stood united against him.

However, his lovely and loving mother and the restful, welcoming rural setting of their lives provided comfort and stimulation that soon dispelled the dread aura of disaster. There was lots of time and plenty of places in which to play—and to think with no sense of combat or confusion. His mother loved the woods, all nature. The friends of the forest were her friends—all was one to her in some indefinable manner, and spoke to her of God and of a Some Day land that was perfect, compellingly majestic and personal. She supplemented this spiritual diet with the Holy Scriptures and a spontaneous telling of Bible stories. Also, Rebecca and little Sam were not indigent. William had owned two houses, in one of which they lived; and there was a widow's pension for dependents of deceased officers of the war, and some income from her father's estate. Further, when William had gone to war, Rebecca had taken his place as teacher and retained that position when he died. It was not a struggling existence nor an unhappy one and Sam grew with a vigorous, athletic body and an inquiring mind. A little later, however, Sam knew the first shock of many to assail him in a short time.

"Sam," said his mother happily, "life is good, isn't it? But do you know what? Soon, it will be much better, for you're going to have a stepfather. He has two fine children, and you'll have great times together!"

The gentleman was a medical doctor, who had great dreams of prosperity and accomplishment. The marriage took place, but the dreams were never realized. Soon Rebecca began to worry about their deteriorating financial condition, and it wasn't long before Sam sensed and indeed overheard what the townspeople thought of the new marriage. They now belonged to the "poor folk" of the community. The new father decided to make a change in lifestyle to become more prosperous. He switched from medicine to farming. The land was the answer! But it was not. Then, perhaps, farming would be better in Indiana, so they removed to Harrison-ville; a little later there was another move to a farm near Shoals, Indiana. Now they were indeed living hand to mouth. Rebecca had no time for leisurely story-telling now, and never a laughing walk through the forest. She looked white and thin and worried. Nevertheless, she kept a watch over her boy and urged him to read and to write and to think marvelous thoughts about the nature of things—and how much God cared and provided. Though farmers' children were needed at home eight or nine months a year, Sam nevertheless learned many things now, truths that trotted beside him like old friends in the years to come, dependable, invigorating, inciting thoughts such as: God is Creator, and we are made in His image; God is love, and we are made to receive that love; God is righteous, and He wants us to be like Him.

He kept reading, listening and looking—looking at nature, looking at himself, studying the few books in his home. While some children memorized the ABCs he began a long literary journey with such friends as *Pilgrim's Progress*, Plutarch's *Lives*, Stephen's *History of Methodism*, Dicken's *Pickwick Papers*, the work of Josephus, Scott's *Ivanhoe*, *Les Miserables* and *History of Our Wars*. And when he tired of these he read Webster's *Unabridged Dictionary*.

"I began to read history very young," he wrote later. "Reading fired my boyish ambition, and determined me some day to make history myself."

He liked the sound of words, combinations of nicely arranged words; he liked the look of them on paper; and he liked the purpose of words—to make people know what was in the minds and hearts of other people. He was fascinated by the truth that thoughts could leap back and forth, enriched, defined, growing like long-legged farmers' children, bright and beautiful and eager. A word has been called "the skin of a living thought," and Sam very early began to regard them as such—pulsing, purposeful, not to be wasted.

By the time he was 12, he knew a lot about words—and life. The best thing of all, he believed, was that he knew he could go on learning, always learning. A new interest gripped him. Always eager for excitement and accomplishment, he became a sturdy part of the sports community of his little Indiana town. "I'll play! Count on me!" Sam wrestled and tugged and scuffled, threw balls and jumped hurdles, ran races. "We want Sam! He's on our side!" was pleasant to his ears. It was a great feeling to have others acclaim you a good contestant—better yet, a winner! And if you set your heart on it—learned how to play, how to judge the other fellow—how to win—why you could do just about anything!

Learn, learn, learn—that was his magic key—and try always to be the best. Learn from nature, from books, from companions, from his own body, his thoughts. Learn from school, from animals, from observation of others. Even learn from church.

Frisky boys traditionally find church confining and more of a bore than a blessing, but there was so much of obvious enthusiasm and merriment, and sweetness that Sam really did not mind—in fact he was intrigued often with the faces and expressions of worshipers when he attended with his stepfather, mother, stepsister, and brother. Church was imperative to most prairie dwellers; inside the sod or wood church walls was all most of them would know of worship, entertainment, education, and socialization. And it was well worth donning stiff Sunday clothes for the enjoyment of happy, handclapping singing, sweet, solemn prayers, strong sermons and best of all, the testimonies from farmers whose lives had been changed powerfully by an experience they called "conversion."

Sam watched these "converts" with wonder—especially farm men, ridden by guilt, fierce mannered, with irate speech and cruel ways, stop their tongues, hold back the heavy hand—and eventually, some of them, develop an attitude so genuinely peaceful that they could not be provoked. Studying them, listening, Sam sometimes felt fear, even terror. He could never make such a change! If he were confronted with the temptations they talked about, he could never withhold himself. He knew he had a violent temper—and some day it would out! As he heard of men driven to drink, and knife slaughter and gunfire when their emotions rose high enough, he cringed in agony. "I'd have to let go!" he'd say to himself. "I'd have to let go!"

One day he grew resentful at his stepfather and shouted his bitterness shrilly. His mother only looked at him, but the pain in her face never left him.

"Her look of grief I can still see across the years," he later recounted. "It was the one sad memory of my childhood. A stranger might have been amused or incensed at my words, but Mother was grieved—grieved to her heart by my lack of generous, self-forgetful, thoughtful love."

In the autumn of 1872, the family moved again, across the Indiana state line about eight miles into Olney, Illinois. Sam sat in church one Sunday, listening to a rather oratorical sermon, fascinated with the whole process of speech, when the minister's face suddenly became "lighted with an unutterable glory." He stared, then an overwhelming thought shook him: *I want to be a Christian!*

He wanted to make his decision known, but no one talked about deciding, so he did nothing. However, several months later, with other boys in the small rural Methodist Episcopal church, sitting on the very last bench, he listened carefully as the minister said, "Come and get religion! Come, stand at the altar rail!"

Sam hurried to the altar rail. He had no idea what to say or how to pray at such a time, so he listened to those nearby.

"God, deliver my soul!"

"I confess I am a sinner!"

"In the name of Jesus Christ, save me!"

He repeated everything he heard and then waited for the lightning bolt of Divinity which would shake and shatter and finally save him. But nothing came. Five successive nights he knelt at the "mourners' bench," feeling not much of anything, certainly not a sense of sinfulness. Just the urge to be God's boy.

I wonder, he thought, *why God doesn't make me feel something? Where is my big experience?* He remained kneeling, but the weather being quite hot and the room stifling, he dropped off to sleep while dutifully kneeling. And this more than once. On Christmas Eve, which was his fifth night, Sam's mother knelt beside him.

"Sam," she said, putting her arms around him, "now that you have come forward publicly and given yourself to God, you can trust." Sam agreed and rose. He was asked to testify about his remarkable experience but he didn't know what to say so he used words from statements others had made.

Weeks passed and no divine constellation proclaimed his salvation, and no star shone in his spirit. He felt the same as he ever had. One night while walking with his mother to prayer meeting, he mentioned another proposed move by the family.

"I'm glad we didn't move to Texas, Mother," he said. "If we had I might have fallen in with rough fellows and lost my soul. But we stayed here and I became a Christian."

An inexplicable sense of peace shot through him—of rightness, of goodness. All was well. Months of this marvelous sense of peace ensued and Sam was overjoyed. Then something happened that totally unnerved him and although he knew he was not out of God's love, still there was something coiled in serpentine fashion ready to strike, something he recognized could thwart, even strangle him. He had been told he could be like Jesus, yet when the incident happened, he met a part of himself that certainly was not like Jesus—exactly the opposite, in fact. A boy had taunted him, called him an objectionable name, and Sam was furious. Prairie rules demanded that either the aggressor retract or there ensued a fight. There was no retraction so Sam hit him—hard. The boy ran and nothing came of the incident outwardly but for Sam "the inward light had gone out." The lightheartedness had disappeared. There was no smile in his soul.

"I'm sorry, I'm sorry, I'm sorry," pled Sam to God and to his mother, but it was some time before the shock of his will to strike anything or anybody which hurt him was subdued and something of peace returned; however, he carried with him knowledge of his potential for aggression which could make him act in opposition to all he desired to be. Could a fellow never be sure he could be good, godly?

About this time a leading man in the community became interested in Sam and, chatting with him about theological subjects, soon detected Sam's chief weakness.

"Your great difficulty will be a burning impatience in regard to little things," he said. "You'll want to do great things."

He was right, and Sam's first thought of entering the ministry proved him so. "I was a bright Bible student even as a child, and a little Pharisee," testified Sam later. "And it came one day to me in the old chapel, listening to an eloquent, imposing preacher that it would be a grand thing to be a minister." It was a transient if indicative thought, and Sam gave much more attention to the sense of disturbance, even violence within.

If I keep very, very busy, I can manage quite well, Sam thought. And so he did. Also, this left him less time to consider many other matters that were beginning to claim thought. He yearned for some formula that would give him complete self control. He got very busy with innumerable good things—he threw himself into religious activity—Bible reading, Sunday school lessons, prayer preparation. And when at 15 he was asked to substitute for his absent Sunday school teacher, he did a creditable job, soon after

being asked to become assistant Sunday school superintendent.
Now the sense of responsibility grew. Now he would *have* to be
good. The fury on the inside must go. Everything unlike God must
go. He'd have none of it. He would rid himself completely of his
explosive nature. *I must be strong. I must overcome. I must not stagger or
stumble.*

Strong boy, Sam Brengle. The drive to excel was growing in
him, breathlessly galloping along with his will to be good. He began
to concentrate on his studies, and in 1874 enrolled in Olney High
School, an achievement in itself, where his immense interest in
words, "meanings, phrases and sentences that set the mind singing
and aching as do the melodies of an orchestra," helped him discipline
himself. After a year in high school, Sam, through his teachers,
met a Professor Hinman at Claremont, about seven miles from
Olney, who was a specialist in words and phrases. For two years,
Hinman housed, fed and taught Sam, with paternal affection and
demanding expectation.

"At that time," remembered Sam, "I decided I could make my
mark in the world as a lawyer. Lawyer I would be." However, one of
his teachers sternly counseled, "Sam, you'll go to hell as sure as you
take to law. You're cut out to be a minister!"

Sam learned well but, still only 14, he got tremendously homesick. It was a long seven miles home and visits were never frequent
enough. When he had studied two years with Professor Hinman,
he was suddenly overwhelmed with a desire to see his mother so
he made the journey and had a memorable visit during a weekend,
riding off to the Professor again on Sunday.

As he mounted his horse, his mother called, "Be a good boy,
won't you, Sammy."

He waved. The following Wednesday, a telegram urged: "Come
quick. Mother dying," but before he reached home, she was dead.

Professor Hinman welcomed him back into his home, offered

comfort in his grief, and the succor of deeper learning, but this no longer sufficed. Sam needed wider horizons now. He was restive and curious and brokenhearted. He must keep moving. He must keep learning. He must succeed in a big way. One day his name would be known to thousands upon thousands of people. Sam Brengle would make good! There was some money left by his own father. He must think. He must be practical. After all, he wasn't penniless. His stepfather held the guardianship of money left for him. College!

"I need it for college," he told his stepfather. "This is very important."

"Waste of time and money," stated his stepfather and would not release it. Very soon after, the stepfather moved away without notice, taking Sam's money with him. Sam was disturbed but not distraught. There must be a way. The farm remained. That was it!

He sold the farm and with the profit realized in the fall of 1877 enrolled at Indiana Asbury University (changed in 1882 to DePauw University), spending two years in preparatory work before matriculating for college. He wanted to do all the right things to insure success. He applied himself to his studies. He handed in his church letter and put himself on record as a Christian. He was given leadership of a large Sunday school class. He was made president of the college YMCA. He also took an active part in extracurricular activities, including the college lyceum for religious discussion, and soon became expert in one field—oratory. He enjoyed thinking; he enjoyed words and their power, and he enjoyed expressing thought. He also reveled in the appreciative, sometimes stunning response his speaking got. Maybe *this* would be how he would make a name for himself.

Christianity and oratory ought to do very well together. Many others had made them work to great advantage. This was the Victorian day of florid ornamentation both in dress and speech.

This was America's day of the orator—both secular and religious. The American public was dazzled and dizzied with verbal eloquence. The most popular man in any profession was the man who used words profusely—colorful, stylized, bombastic, and many folk in America, the land of abundance, seemed to use more words than were needed, as they used other bounty.

During the 1880's, having finally liberated the black man, the United States was indulgently eager to liberate herself and sought to escape every possible restriction. Americans built an enormous variety of private and public buildings, characterized by rococo ornamentation as extravagant as bulging purses would permit. There were multiple ways in which to spend money: private "Pullman" palaces (trains), investments, and the use of newly-invented miracles such as typewriters, high-wheeled bicycles, incandescent lamps, and the "lover's telegraph," the telephone. Marvelous innovations were being made in a basically agricultural society, especially in farm implements and machinery. The streets were still lighted by gas, but horsecars were replacing locomotives and mail-order houses brought treasures to the nation's doorstep. Indians had lost their battle with the white man in a last dramatic stand when they massacred General George Custer and 264 of his men at the Little Big Horn on June 25, 1876. The Ku Klux Klan was involved in fiery declarations of fury, and the common people were beginning to rebel, showing their intent in organized groups. Women were speaking in noisy demonstrations.

Immigrants from southern Europe clogged into the States and joined with discharged soldiers of the War between the States moving west where there was plenty of room to grow with their dreams. There was also phenomenal growth in the border cities of the east, where workers without money or job skills settled as machinists and mill workers. Coal, oil, and steel made multi-millionaire barons of determined and sometimes unrighteous men. It was the day of Jay Gould, Jim Fisk, Andrew Carnegie,

William K. Vanderbilt, John D. Rockefeller, and of the meat-packing kings: Swift, Hormel, and Cudahy. The 1880's also hailed the new journalism, with editors intent on circulation, often at the expense of truth—and certainly of balance. Reporters snooped for scoops.

The machine age had begun, and henceforth America would depend on money for its measurement of success and gentility. Great wealth bred enormous poverty. No one as yet related Christianity seriously to responsibility for the deprived and depraved. Token gestures were made in the breadline, but the God who seemed to cajole the rich seemed not a blood-relative to the waifs, widows, and wild-eyed drunks who soiled the seam on the garment of silken Victorian society in America.

By many this period was called the Golden Age; others referred to it as gilded. Sometimes the gilt seemed already to be chipping and the frame of society cracking. But it was a bright, if impossible picture in that frame—gaudily representative of a promised land for which so many hearts yearned: a land of milk and honey.

This was the world of Sam Brengle. Sam studied oratory, orators; he formulated and he rehearsed. He won prizes in his college and for it. He spent hours at piano and organ, pounding out the notes of the scale and matching them with his voice, developing a melodic resonant tone, striving for control, flexibility, and beauty. He was invited to join Delta Kappa Epsilon fraternity and represented his school in state competitions—as important in that day as is college football competition today. A great way to become famous, Sam concluded.

He enjoyed the lyceum.[1] It indulgently stirred the coals of his imagination—and his tongue. And it was with this group that he first heard of a strange inner experience.

---

1. A college group, with invited ministers, which met regularly for religious discussion.

"The first time I ever heard of completely pure living (holiness) was in that lyceum," he told Elizabeth soon after they met. "The ministers of the town all belonged to it, and at one meeting a hungry junior asked of the wiseacres present if one could not be delivered from all sin. One of the professors who was in the chair quoted a certain bishop who said that deliverance came by growth, and that ended the matter. I regarded it as a church doctrine and wasn't interested in it."

The next year Sam began reading Comte and Harrison, and soon found himself in a skeptical fog. "But I held on to a form of godliness," he remembered. "It was impossible to get away from my mother's teaching unless I went deeper far into sin, and her memory kept me from that."

During summer vacation he stayed in town, read, loafed, and became even more religiously skeptical. In his third year, he definitely decided to study law, wanting "a home, and chances for worldly preferment which I couldn't find elsewhere, for the outcome of my ambition was to be a public speaker. I loved to prepare and elaborate orations, and when I took part in an oratorical contest would rather have died than not win. In short, I was given over to selfishness and love of acclaim."

Then revival swept through the town. In one meeting a young woman spoke of what she called spiritual consecration. "You must give all of yourself to God," she said and invited the students to the altar rail. Sam went. Give all? What had he not given? All he could think of was law, and law he presented. The following day the invitation was given again. Another student rose to testify that he had been afraid that if he consecrated himself, God would call him to the desert—maybe to be a missionary!

Right! said Sam to himself. *That's exactly it. Maybe I'll be called* to missionary service if I give my all. Shuddering but desperate for inner peace, he gave himself to God for Asia, Africa, anywhere. Hate it or not, he *had* to choose God's way. After that, he had considerable power in his preaching, but never got beyond selfishness in his personal life. *Must win! Must win!* "I went in for honors as hard as ever, and winning them made me no better," he recounted. "In my last college year, I heard again of a special experience. One of the fellows who had got it testified to it, and his life bore it out. He got some of the boys into the experience and came and prayed with me. But he *prayed too loud.* I couldn't wait for him to be done. I was afraid someone else would know there was prayer going on in my room. Still, I lived nearer to God after that and had peace with Him—but it was far from the peace of God *in me.*"

During his last term as an undergraduate, something occurred that changed Sam's life forever. Trouble had risen in the nationwide fraternity, and due to Sam's bargaining ability, he was sent east to solicit support for his chapter, which was in danger of being dropped. On his way to the convention which was to be held in Providence, R.I. he stopped off at many colleges along the way but was told repeatedly, "We'll fight you to the death!"

Where lay the answer? Sam considered all alternatives. Prayer. Certainly God would attend to the matter. He prayed earnestly three times but got no assurance or sense of self-confidence. Only more interior struggle, more anxiety. Finally, he pled, "Oh Lord, if You'll help me win this case, I'll preach!"

What kind of bargain was that? Nevertheless, he jumped to his feet, lighthearted. And he won.

"So you see, Bev,[2] old boy," he explained to a student friend, "I've got to preach!" to which the perturbed friend exploded, "Sam, you'll be a fool to go into the ministry!"

But Sam's mind was made up. On returning to school, he

---

2. "Bev" was Sam's nickname for Albert Jeremiah Beveridge who later became widely known as an orator. He became a U.S. senator and the biographer of John Marshall, Abraham Lincoln, and others.

immediately started noon-day prayer meetings. Revival broke out; he took preaching engagements that attracted attention and got the promise of a ministerial appointment. So far so good.

After receiving his bachelor of arts degree in 1884, Sam, now the Reverend Samuel Logan Brengle, A.B., served for a year as a circuit preacher of the Methodist Episcopal Church, then decided to get more training and attend a theological seminary. He wanted to explore the east coast and big city life, so he enrolled in Boston Theological Seminary, then one of the three great Methodist seminaries in America.

At Boston he outlined a course of study which would "have wrecked" him, he later commented. "I spent a lot of time in art study as well, but the best hour of every day was given to the Bible and prayer. That saved me."

His sense of industry and earnestness were not new—his growing anxiety about his spiritual condition was. He threw himself into study. Fellow students, curious, would remark, "Still at it Brengle? We see your light burning when we go to bed and it's still burning when we get up!" Sam never mentioned the real driving force, that since 12, he'd been often in terror of the propensity for evil inside himself. Through the years he'd read everything he could find, conversed with everyone who would converse with him regarding a mature and blameless spiritual experience. But nothing to date had ever satisfied him.

Next, he tried the Octogon Club, a college group subscribing to daily communal prayer and discussion. He began serious study under Professor Daniel Steele, then professor of Didactic Theology at Boston University and one of the world's foremost authorities on the Greek New Testament. And he went on collecting and reading all the material he could find dealing with the spirit of man in relation to the Spirit of God. Especially intriguing but somewhat incomprehensible were the writings of an English-woman who, with her husband, had recently founded a novel religious organization called The Salvation Army—Catherine Booth. She wrote about woman's right to express herself publicly, especially in religious proclamation, and she wrote about something she called "a clean heart."

Described by teacher, preacher, and writer, Sam reflected, there was apparently a spiritual experience that settled a Christian, turned all his tendencies toward God, rooted out the inherent ugliness of his nature; freed him of anxiety, gave him power over the seeds of conflict, helped him realize that it was not the manifestation of sin that was the chief enemy of men's souls, but the willful, self-intentioned spirit behind the deed.

Some termed this experience "sanctification," some "holiness," "perfect love," "second work of grace," "baptism of (and by) the Holy Spirit," "blessing of a clean heart," "the higher-up religion." Some submitted that "holiness" actually meant "wholeness," that God meant his beings to be joyful, lighthearted, overcoming, but that in the use of a self-controlled free will, humankind had, naturally, gone its own way—yet always with an inner yearning for God, and that conscious return of the will to God was the only way to know peace and righteousness.

That Sam was a Christian he did not dispute. That he was not altogether at ease in Christianity he knew also. Something certainly was still lacking in him. He looked to Jesus for his model and began to loathe himself, even the goodness, the education, the proficiency he had worked so hard to attain.

He took charge of Egleston Square Church, Boston, while going on with theology and art. Here his spiritual hunger and dissatisfaction grew until body and spirit seemed to be torn apart, and he got ill. While overwrought, he heard of a "holiness" meeting and attended. The songs, the faces of the people struck him with conviction.

I want what they've got! Sam kept telling himself. *I'd better go forward. You're making a fool of yourself if you do,* a voice said within. *That's no place for a man known as a responsible pastor.* But Sam went, confessed, believed, and found peace. If he had held fast to his profession, all would have been well, but the next day reproaches of others troubled him. Said Sam later: "I sought the blessing and was richly blessed but I did not *get the blessing* and the blessing I did receive leaked out. 'I struggled and wrestled to win it, the blessing that setteth me free.' But I did not see the way of faith and indeed I do not now think that I was prepared for the *inner crucifixion* which enables one to believe unto holiness of heart." He lost his self-confidence and sank into despair that made him physically ill.

"I hated the I in me," he said of this experience. He wanted to give great things to God, to be important to God and for Him. Next, even that beat on his consciousness. "I'll take the meanest little appointment there is! Please, God!" If only he could have the experience of victory! He'd be noble. He'd be eloquent. He'd be marvelously self-disciplined. What deeds he'd do for God! No, no, not that! *Do* for God? "Oh, Lord," he finally said, "I wanted to be an eloquent preacher, but if by stammering and stuttering I can bring greater glory to you than by eloquence, then let me stammer and stutter."

Self renunciation. Self denial. Self revelation. Now! Now, God would honor him with the supreme assurance, some remarkable experience of cleansing. But nothing happened.

He knelt, feeling altogether filthy. Then, it seemed, all the sins man ever had committed were part of him. Then even his good seemed terrifying evil. His public speaking. Ugh! God showed him how he'd put brilliant periods and swelling climaxes in his sermons to glorify himself, that he'd been giving the people rhetoric and philosophy and his own ideas—putting himself between the people and Christ Jesus. "Oh, my God," Sam prayed, "If You'll give me a clean heart, I'll give the people Your unadorned truth always!"

But his evil kept jumping up before him. Even his prayers had been wrong—all wrong. He'd been delightedly conscious of their eloquence!

"He showed me stark selfishness," Sam remembered. "That while I wanted to go into the law for worldly preferment and power, and had given that up, yet now I had come to want ecclesiastical preferment. If I couldn't have place in the world, then I'd have place in the church. I had given up being a great lawyer, a wealthy legislator, to seek fame as a pulpit orator! I had thought I was unselfish when I had offered to bury myself in Singapore. But God asked me now if I'd be willing to take a mean little appointment in the church."

"Yes," Sam pled, "only give me peace!"

He felt as if he were being pressed completely out of himself. Out, out to nothing. Tempting thoughts jabbed like ladies' hatpins all over his body.

You'll lose your mind over all this! Give it up! You're going crazy, Sam!

"No!" cried Sam. "I'll see this through. I'll see it through! Go ahead, God!"

God then showed him his neglect of little duties, things he'd never thought of before, of eating and drinking for the glory of God, or of the literal meaning of "Whatsoever ye do, in word or deed, *do all in the Name of the Lord Jesus.*" But an indefinable bright white light began to shine into him—he began to *know* curiously that his highest good and God's highest glory were identical!

"Many times since," Sam told Elizabeth, "I have found myself in places where the old brilliant literary or artistic talk that I used to delight in was going on, but I have had to sit silent and appear stupid, for God shut my mouth once for all to everything not to His glory. I was right in the refiner's fire now, but I cried, 'Lord, don't let me draw back. Don't let me be deceived. I want to get through and know it. Jesus was made of no reputation. He left the highest throne and took the lowest place. He became a Servant of servants, apparently deserted by God. I *will* follow

Jesus! I mean practically. He depended completely upon Your will—You. I want You, too!'"

Are you willing to bury yourself in the north end of Boston? And never see a soul saved?

"Yes.

Will you do without any outward assurance?

Without proof? No one would know he had any power at all that way. *Oh.* Now all his hopes were gone, all ambitions, longings were crushed.

Only believe! But he couldn't. He saw only how restricting, how ugly, how burdening was his unbelief. He knelt for three hours but got no assurance of God taking over his life. Several days later despair was still blanketing Sam. He could think of little, do little, enjoy nothing, no one at all. Self disgust made his whole life a putrid vomit on his person. At the end of his fretting and failing, flailing and wailing, offering and offending, his making deals with God, he simply gave up. Immediately to his mind flashed an excerpt of Scripture:

"If we confess our sins, He is faithful and just to forgive us our sins—" then the other hemisphere of truth dawned upon him: "and to cleanse us *from all unrighteousness.*"

"Lord, I believe that," said Sam simply. And he did. That was all. Quick as a breath the Spirit of God said, "Yes, Sam!" and the deed was done. Peace settled within him.

Immediately, student friends noticed a difference.

"Sam, what's the matter. You look so different!"

"Sam, the moment I saw you I said to myself, something's happened to Brengle."

The next morning, while walking across Boston Commons, he met a carriage driver friend who lived this peaceful life and when Sam described his new possession, the driver exulted, "Preach it, Sam! Preach it!"

Sam decided to do just that and the next day, in Egleston Square

church where he was student pastor, he did. Two mornings later
the powerful faith "engine of the Lord" was hitched to loaded
boxcars of God's manifold experiential treasures which Sam had
found:

I awoke that morning hungering and thirsting just to live this life of
fellowship with God. Getting out of bed about six o'clock with that desire,
I opened my Bible and while reading some of the words of Jesus, He gave
me such a blessing as I never had dreamed a man could have this side of
heaven. It was an unutterable revelation. It was a heaven of love that came
into my heart. My soul melted like wax before fire. I sobbed. I walked out
over Boston Commons before breakfast, weeping for joy and praising
God. Oh, how I loved. In that hour I knew Jesus, and I loved Him till it
seemed my heart would break. I was filled with love for all His creatures. I
heard the little sparrows chattering. I loved them. I saw a little worm
wriggling across my path; I stepped over it; I didn't want to hurt any living
thing. I loved the dogs. I loved the horses. I loved the little urchins on the
street. I loved the strangers who hurried past me. I loved the heathen. I
loved the whole world!

In time God withdrew some of the tremendous emotional feelings. He taught Sam that he had to live by faith and not by
emotions. But he walked in a blaze of glory for weeks. The glory
gradually subsided, and Sam learned that he had to trust God—no
matter how he felt. But now there was assurance that he could.

Not long after, when Sam expressed himself, many of the old
theological friends pled for caution, correction, some even cancel-
lation. "Brother Brengle," they cautioned, "that doctrine splits
churches!"

As indeed it had, and did, and does today.[3]

---

3. In the preface to Brengle's first book and later reprinted many times, Bramwell
Booth, second general of The Salvation Army, wrote: "In no department of its
teaching has The Salvation Army suffered more reproach than in this—of "Holiness unto the Lord." Indeed, its teaching as distinct from its methods, has, apart
from this, been largely welcomed by every section of the professing church. . . .
Our witness to entire sanctification has done much to preserve us, for it has

But Sam was sure of himself now and he witnessed openly to this maturity of spirit, however, not altogether in the manner of most other "Holiness" preachers of his time. Sensitive himself, he had no reliance upon emotion; he did not command nor demand "tongues"; he decried a religion without reason, or reason without religion, and he seriously wondered if this key could be made popular at any time. Yet he felt no misgivings. He was as determined, earnest, hard-working, and lighthearted as ever. The great difference seemed to be in his settled faith, his sense of inner peace—and his lightheartedness.

Then another unscheduled event happened, something that seemed at the time entirely happenstance. During the autumn of 1885, William Booth, founder of The Salvation Army, visited America. During October of 1884, Major Thomas Moore, leader of Army forces in the United States, had decided that the Salvation Army must become an independent national force and had organized revolutionary forces, incorporated and left the ranks, taking most of the soldiery with him. The Army was near disaster. A divisional leader, Major Annie Shirley (who with her husband and daughter Eliza had founded the work in the States in 1879), now widowed, and one of a few loyal leaders, was administrating from Boston, where she had "opened fire" a month before the schism. The ranks were split asunder. There had been devastating publicity in the press, and brutal physical abuse by roughs,

---

aroused opposition, not merely from the intellectual apologists for existing systems, but also from the thousands whose half-hearted service and unwilling consecration it has condemned.

The holiness we contend for is a fighting holiness, a suffering holiness, a soul-saving holiness; in short, Jesus Christ's holiness. Any mere "enjoyment of religion," "waiting on God" or "fullness of blessing" which has not immediately and indissolubly joined with it, in every expression of it, the most unselfish and aggressive passion for the rescue of sinners from their sins, is, in our judgment, a mere caricature of the higher life of complete union with Christ, which the word of God declares to be the highest life of all."

churchmen, and saloonkeepers. In a resuscitation effort, William Booth visited Boston, spoke in several places, including a minor hall in Tremont Temple, to students, many of whom were openly disdainful and accusative. However, as Sam Brengle watched, he felt the tapping of destiny.

"The door opened," he wrote later. "A man entered. It was the tall, gaunt form of the Army's founder. He had a long beard and his dark blue military tunic was open, exposing a flaming red guernsey (sweater) on which were the words: BLOOD AND FIRE. I burst into tears at sight of him."

Booth compelled the attention of his youthful audience, and as Brengle shook his hand, Sam murmured, apparently unheard, "I wish I could join you." However, Booth went home to England and Sam went back to his studies until graduation. At that time, two offers were made to him. A tempting one came from South Bend, Indiana, where Clement Studebaker, millionaire wagon builder, had built a new church and Sam had been recommended as pastor. Here his oratorical skill and magnetic preaching ability would help make him a popular minister. But Sam now felt a call to evangelistic preaching, and decided to go on preaching "on the field of human need." Infrequently he would observe the black-clad soldiers of The Salvation Army marching and singing, taunted and tormented, and a small aching voice inside would adjure, *Look! Listen! Your people, Sam. Your people.*

APPENDIX

Ancestry

The Brengle family's sojourn in the United States dates back to prerevolutionary days. Samuel's great grandparents being George Brengle, born February 16, 1762; and Susan born July 14, 1775. One of the offspring of this union, George D., emigrated from Maryland to

Washington County, Kentucky, and sired the following children, plus two whose names are unknown:

George Washington	b. Dec. 19, 1819
Elizabeth	b. May 16, 1818
James Perry	b. Nov. 25, 1822, Presbyterian minister
Joshua	b. 1824, medical doctor
Mary Louisa	b. 1828, married Samuel S. Marshall
John	b. 1830
Jefferson	served in Union Army
Logan	
William Nelson	served in Union Army; wife, Rebecca Horner; father of Samuel Logan

Brengle's Favorite Poet

That Alfred Lord Tennyson was Brengle's favorite poet is evident from Brengle's much-marked copy of Tennyson's poetry. The volume is filled with notations, underlinings, even a correction to suit Brengle's belief. Beneath his name on the flyleaf is this quotation from *The Battle Hymn of the Republic:*

> *He hath sounded forth the trumpet that shall never call retreat;*
> *He is sifting out the hearts of men before His judgment seat;*
> *O be swift my soul to answer Him; be jubilant my feet.*
> *Our God is marching on!*

Here are a few of the many underlined passages:

> That man's the best cosmopolite
> Who loves his native country best.

> That man's the true conservative,
> Who lops the moulder'd branch away.

> I am a part of all that I have met.

> As the husband is, the wife is:
> Thou art mated with a clown;
> And the grossness of his nature will
>   have weight to drag thee down.

> Slander, meanest spawn of hell,
> And women's slander is the worst.

That men may rise on stepping stones
Of their dead selves to higher things.

Thy woes are birds of passage, transitory

Like men, like manners; like breeds like, they say;
Kind nature is the best; those manners best
That fit us like a nature second hand;
Which are indeed the manners of the great.

I myself must mix with action,
Lest I wither by despair.

With the creeping hours
That lead me to my Lord,
Make Thou my spirit pure and clear,
As are the frosty skies;
Or this first snowdrop of the year
That in my bosom lies.

For words, like nature, half reveal
And half conceal the soul within.

But oh for the touch of a vanished hand,
And the sound of a voice that is still!
. . . But the tender grace of a day that is dead
Will never come back to me.

You are bones, and what of that?
Every face, however full,
Padded round with flesh and fat,
Is but modeled on a skull.

The path of duty was the way to glory.

Our little systems have their day;
They have their day and cease to be;
They are but broken lights of thee,
And Thou, O Lord, are more than they.

My strength is as the strength of ten
Because my heart is pure.

Great deeds cannot die;
They with the sun and moon renew their light
Forever, blessing those that look on them.

Cursed be the social wants that sin
   against the strength of youth!
Cursed be the social lies that warp us
   from the living truth!
Cursed be the sickly forms that err
   from honest nature's rule;
Cursed be the gold that gilds the straightened
   forehead of the fool!

So runs my dream, but what am I?
An infant crying in the night;
An infant crying for the light;
And with no language but a cry.

Two

Elizabeth Swift

When Sam Brengle strode into an evening service in a Boston church during the summer of 1885, he was unprepared for what he found. It was disturbing enough to listen to a woman speak publicly and with authority, but to hear a woman *preach* was societally unacceptable—and such a woman! Somehow he had anticipated more bone, more muscle.

"I can see her still," he recalled years later, "as she stood that night before a critical and only half sympathetic audience—a slender, delicate, cultured woman—and preached the truth as I had seldom, if ever, heard it preached, in language simple yet delicately refined, and searching as a fire to the consciences of men."

What's more, her message centered on the possibility and practicality of a wholesome, even "holy" relationship of a man with his God. Sam looked, listened, and fell in love with Lily Swift fully and forever.

"I lost my heart," Sam explained. "But not my head." He went out of the service determined to be cautious, no matter what state of palpitation his pulse was in. In matters of love involving marriage, he was persuaded that "head and heart should keep pace with each other. There should be not only love, which is a passion of the heart, but also profound respect and intellectual sympathy, which are largely matters of the head."

Though his heart "had the first innings," he immediately proposed to give his head a chance. So the next morning he wrote Elizabeth "Lily" Swift a letter and began a correspondence which did not end until there was no little hand to lift a pen and begin, "My darling Sam."

Still, to imagine that there immediately was begun a torrid romance that led straightway to marriage is ludicrously far from the truth, for though Sam was certain, Lily hadn't the slightest interest in marital bliss. Indeed, in many respects, she represented the new breed of American young ladies: society belle, determined on equal rights for women, even to the exclusion of marriage. She had refinement, education, a passion for integrity and money behind her.

Lily Swift was no ordinary girl. That she had become a "preaching woman" was proof of that, and that she espoused a tenet of doctrine that admittedly stirred up dissension and often confusion described her temperament and ability still more precisely. But when the fact of extreme physical frailty is added, the picture is of a young woman as singular, magnetic, intellectual, and purposeful as Catherine Booth, co-founder of The Salvation Army. The role these women played in later years differed immensely, and the significance of the two, comparatively and contrastingly, is part of the purpose of this record.

An observation made after Lily's death by Florence Bramwell Booth, wife of the second General of The Salvation Army, seems so unlike Lily as to be inappropriate: "Mrs. Brengle's life reminds us of the humble sweetness and yet dignity of the violet." Lily Swift was no violet! Then why the comparison? How apply it? Young Lily was about as quiet as a peacock and shrinking as a rose. Also, she possessed a genuine sweetness and gaiety in her love of life that brought the bees winging wherever she adorned the countryside.

Tiny Lily came into the lives of George Henry and Pamela (long E) Swift on July 23, 1849, in ideal surroundings. She was born in Amenia, New York, in a manorly colonial home, among sprawling farmlands, framed by mountains. Her father was a banker with a law background, who like many others of the Victorian era lived pleasantly as a gentleman farmer in the country and worked as a business-professional leader in the city. Lily with her younger sister Susie (four other children died in infancy) lived in a child's paradise—with every kind of rural delight accessible: swimming and fishing, horseback riding; cows and calves, chickens, pigs, and turkeys; and the companionship of several cousins who lived nearby.

Lily's father was affectionate, thoughtful, and indulgent, her mother affectionate and protective. And though four other children in the family died, Lily and Susie seemed to accept the bereavement philosophically and to live happy, normal lives, with one exception—perhaps subconsciously tied to the death experience and the Victorian preachment of that day—*Lily was terrified of going to hell.*

Serious thought is still, by some, discredited in small children but Lily knew what she thought and when she thought it, and so did her parents. And she knew what torture came to her when, at five, she learned to read and quickly absorbed the Westminster Catechism of the Calvinist belief of her parents. The doctrine of the "elect," subscribed to was enormously satisfying—if you were one of God's elect. But how could you tell? What if you weren't? Coupled with that problem was a growing conviction that people were responsible for themselves, that anybody could do just about anything he wanted to and be anybody he wanted to be—if he really truly wanted to. She discussed the matter with her friend Lila.[1]

---

1. A fictitious name. Lily rarely used actual names in her writings.

"How do you know you belong to God?"

"Oh, Lily, silly. Because you're elect!"

"Am I?"

"Of course!"

"Why?"

"Because of the witness of the Spirit."

"The what?"

"Because you're one of the 'lected."

Lily was not satisfied. Not only after, her parents took her with them to hear an evangelist in a neighboring church. When the sermon was finished, the evangelist shouted, "Everybody here who wants to go to heaven, stand right up and the Christians here will pray for you!"

Lily was stunned. Go to Heaven? Of course! She stood. And when she could, she joined that church. However, the whole subject of religion gnawed at her. Nobody seemed to say anything exact about God. And He seemed so far off. Did He send *little* girls to hell? Did He write the Bible all by Himself? She watched and listened. She wanted something a person could count on. Like arithmetic. Or like building a house. You had to know what you were doing. You had to dig down in the earth and make a foundation out of rocks. You had to find some rocks before you built rooms and tore down trees to make walls. She did notice that Aunt Eliza, a member of the family, read her Bible and prayed a long time morning and night. Everybody loved Aunt Eliza, and so did Lily.

I'll do just like her, thought Lily and began to pray and pray and read her Bible. The praying went quite smoothly; there were always a lot of things to confess, but the Bible reading was not so easy, and some years later when she enrolled in college, she was still pondering over the best method of studying the Bible and how to deal with what you found when you did.

She was still concerned with hell but also the matter of Heaven now. She read the Bible through. Then she began with Paul's epistles for careful study, thrilled at the possibility of satisfying living, living without fear or conflict of conscience. But how to attain it? How to follow all of Paul's stringent teaching? How on earth could anybody "put away" all "bitterness, wrath, anger, clamor?" Plainly, she read that those who hate and quarrel, who are envious and self-seeking "shall not inherit the Kingdom of God." And worse, the Bible clearly stated: "He that committeth sin is of the devil."

Lily was a most unusual girl. First of all, though she was often consumed with an appreciation of beauty—beauty of color, of form, of sound, of line and proportion, she early decided that she was not at all beautiful. In fact, she decided, she was quite plain and could never compare with her blond sister who had curls and a round doll face. This was not true, except if concluded when judged from cherubic standards; but interestingly enough, Lily was not a girl for jealousy and appreciated her sister's cameo perfection, daintiness, and charm. Little "Pussy," drew attention, whereas Lily's elfin loveliness did not. She was short, slight, and brown, though she had startling blue eyes. She was very near-sighted and wore glasses. But that there was more to elegance than perfection of feature Lily sensed from babyhood. There was something inside that made a great difference; then there was how you attended to beauty outside yourself; and *then* there was the matter of beauty *on* yourself. What you draped about your very own body was important—color, style, and fit.

Lily was very young when she made a most important discovery regarding clothes. In the 1800's, for informal occasions little boys and girls wore long-sleeved gingham aprons that covered them from neck to knee, a smock-like piece of apparel. They were usually of blue and white for girls and brown and white for boys, differing only in cut at the neckline; girls had a turn-down collar and boys, a straight stand-up one. One morning Lily dashed off in her brother's smock and at recess the other little girls gathered round her.

"Lil, you look different some way." "Lily, what's that you've got on?" "Lily! You've got on one of George's aprons! Did you know that?"

"Yes, I did," said Lily. "I was in such a hurry I couldn't change."

The girls eyed her carefully, analytically, then one commented, "Well, all I've got to say is I'd wear it always if I were you. It's ever so much more becoming. You look pretty!"

"Pretty!" the little girls chanted. "Pretty! Real pretty, Lily, you truly do."

The moment she got home, Lily rushed to a tall tilting mirror and made the grand survey. Absolutely true! She wasn't exactly ravishing but she would truly do quite well—there was a sense of altogetherness. She might have said harmony but she was too young. Staring at her image, she flushed with delight. What had made the difference? The brown and white apron certainly— something about that high neck, and the color. *Well,* thought Lily, *if clothes can make that much difference, most certainly when I grow up, I'll make a serious study of the matter.* She kept her vow and in later years her artistry and interest in costuming were given to God as was all else in her life. She was especially enchanted by costume detail and the significance of color and line. When the adjectives of "pretty," "beautiful" and "charming" were applied to her she'd whisper to herself and sometimes comment to a friend, "Great is the power of correct clothes."

Her taste was eclectic. She knew what suited her type, having spent hours of cold analysis studying herself in the "looking glass." She knew weak and strong points, and never wore an article of dress just because it was pretty or fashionable. In her teen years she was not only the talkative leader of her peers but was also a piquant fashionplate. Aunt Sarah, the cook of the household and special confidante of Lily,[2] attended to her favorite's wardrobe personally:

---

2. In daughter Elizabeth's words: "Duchess County, N.Y., had for years been favorable to slaves." Aunt Sarah and her family had been Swift family members since Lily's childhood, Aunt Sarah making an invaluable contribution to Lily's life.

She shore was wordly, and proud as the old fellow himself. . . . The clothes dat girl did have, and the washin'! It makes me tired still to think of them ruffled petticoats of hern, all little weeny, teeny edged ruffles, clear up to the waist. . . . Mebbe she was not a beauty, but she always looked so pretty, and folks made an awful lot of her, parties and dances, an' nothin' else was right from here to Sharon without Miss Lily was in it.

Apparently it was more a sense of concentrated attention on and appreciation of all life that accounted for Lily's interest in clothes. Years later, Sam wrote of her:

She taught me to see beauty everywhere. I came from the middle west, where my grandfather helped to build a fort to protect the settlers from marauders. These people were generally too busy wrestling with the great forests and struggling to build up homes and rear their large families to see the wondrous beauties all about them, but Lily made me see and feel beauty in every fence corner, tangled thicket, fleecy cloud and murmuring brook. Her delight over all these beauties was infectious, and I caught some of her spirit.

More than anyone else, she taught me to see worth and vast possibilities in degraded and neglected souls . . . she introduced me to the poverty-stricken, the ignorant, the pagan in our midst, and made me see their spiritual value. She saw to it that all the despised and poor of the community were invited to our wedding, and her father's house overflowed that day with all the tatterdemalions of the countryside. . . .

Lily's personality was characterized by three rather contrasting qualities: appreciation of beauty; a sensitive, loving disposition; and very articulate stubbornness. The first has been described; the second made everyone about her lighter in spirit and thus acceptant of her, most of the time at any rate; the third often brought agony, especially in youth. Usually her desire to be charming and agreeable kept her self-willed and somewhat domineering nature in the background, and her will and admirable self-control kept a blazing

---

Daughter Elizabeth grew up on tales Lily told her about Aunt Sarah, and especially remembers Aunt Sarah's counsels delivered with the aid of "a warm drop cookie."

temper well in hand. Not always, though. Once, because she had spoken abruptly to her horseman, her father said she must apologize or she could not ride until she did, and Lily forewent that pleasure for an extended period. The second quality resulted in enormous popularity. Of it Aunt Sarah remarked, "She was always dat pleasant, and all the girls we had in the house said jest the same. It was always, 'Thank you, Sarah!' and 'Please, Sarah,' and 'If you'll be so kine.' She had a good, kine heart."

Illustrative of her loving nature and inherent eagerness to help is the incident when little Helen, one of her cousins, suffered so much from toothache that the family agreed that the offending tooth must be pulled. Helen was terrified.

"Look here, Helen," said Lily, not yet seven years old. "If you'll come and have that tooth out, I'll go with you and have one out too, and I'll have mine out first and then you'll see it's not so bad."

Which she did.

"All the way home," said Helen later, "I kept thinking could I do such a thing for somebody else? But that was Lily."

In school, Lily was an excellent student, quick to learn, adept at memorization, and eager to express herself. She was particularly interested in literature and philosophy, counting most poets of the period as her friends. She loved to have a good time, doting on sports and horseback riding, and she loved to lead intellectually, using legalistic persuasion as did her father. She had a great urge to be liked, and soon found ways to manipulate others for this purpose. "None of us cousins could talk her down!" a cousin remembered. Her mind was curious, fed by her father's library and his attitude toward small questioning girls. Her delight in life and eagerness to explore kept her breezily occupied in early years, and there seemed to be no mar on her pleasure-filled young life—except that sometimes gripping fear of hell that had beset her since she could remember anything at all.

She enrolled in college at 16 and became absorbed in campus life:

excellent professors, lots of friends, a whirlwind social life. Occasionally she attempted further inquiry into matters of religion. Once, a "church girl" student asked if she were a church member.

"Yes," said Lily.

"I mean of my church," said the girl. "We don't count any others. If you don't belong to our church you're not a member at all."

Lily was shocked but also interested.

"Tell me about it."

She was then introduced to sectarian doctrine, apostolic succession, the difference between regular and irregular baptism, post and premillennialism, etc. After the discourse, Lily was silent, then she said, "Does it make you good?"

"What do you mean?"

"Does it make you keep your temper and do all the hard things the Bible says you must?"

"Nonsense! No one does that!" said the girl.

And that was that. Lily decided she was too young to be a real Christian. Some day she'd investigate the entire matter. But she could not keep transient thoughts from the death and hell subjects. What if? Years later she commented on this period in her life: "The fear of death is an indestructible safeguard which God has set in our natures to protect the soul."

For Lily the winter of 18 was one of enchantment, if you enjoyed the American Victorian definition: belled horses pulling ornate carriages, mountains of snow and ice, skating parties terminating before cavernous fireplaces of the genteel. If you were a Vassar girl. Especially if your name was Lily Swift. In mid-winter, just at the height of the season, near-tragedy changed life forever for Lily. A skate-strap broke while she was skating, she caught a chill and became critically ill. She was ordered home. Months later the family physician said that heart damage and other complications would prevent Lily from returning to college, that, in fact, she would never be active again. Lily stared at him. An invalid? Never!

"I'll stay home for a year," she announced. "But then I'm going back to college." But she never went back. After a while she philosophically accepted her physical restrictions, and for more than ten years enjoyed life. With sufficient rest in between, she began to take advantage of the cultural and social life about her: books, music, art, society, scientific lectures and classical concerts.

"There was nothing in life that seemed good to me that fate did not give me," remembered Lily. Yet something was wrong. When she was quiet, looking at the fringe along the treetops, and at the top of the sky, she became eerily uneasy, afraid.

"The skeleton at my feast was a very literal one. The thought of death and 'in that sleep of death' what dreams might come, was often with me as a black cloud, dimming alike the sun out in the park and the lights in the ballroom."

Lily's introspective, imaginative nature carved up live demons, which seemed to be uncannily reproductive. What if? If that rearing horse ever fell on her; if that white dress were really her shroud; if her soul were scurrying through space like the ailing soul of Faust in Berkioz's "Symphonie," with the demons sure to overtake it; what then? These were the troubled thoughts which marred her pleasure.

"Just in proportion as these unwelcome ideas obtained in my mind I felt myself growing world-weary," wrote Lily of the experience. "Was that the secret of the discontented faces all about me and did others wonder perpetually, as I did occasionally, why they were born, and if life, even at its best, were worth living?" She studied her neighbors to see if any countenance bore marks of peace. "Religion, from which, except in its outward forms, I had long since parted company, must, I was sure, if really lived out satisfy and bring rest. Did it? Only the calm face of the dear aunt at home, and the like look of two others among all the nominal Christians I knew, gave any outward signs of an abiding, inward peace."

She attempted to measure the lives of all the others she knew by the standard of the New Testament as she understood it. They all fell far short, except for the three. However, a little later one died and one became an unbeliever. She felt one victorious person was not sufficient to build a concept on.

"God has no followers," thought Lily. *"How can I be one?"*

Still, in these days she never gave up listening and looking for God—in churches, tracts, sermons, theological works and religious papers. Nothing captured her heart *and* her head. Then, in 1884, came an avalanche of compelling new experience. Susie, Lily's little sister, had graduated from Vassar in 1883 and instead of relaxing from the strenuous student years, had begun immediately to teach in a fashionable eastern school, eventually collapsing from "nervous breakdown." One day during convalescence she burst in upon Lily.

"Lily! I know just what will make me quite well! A voyage to Europe! Beth[3] and I will go together, and you will come as chaperon! Please, Lily? Please?"

Trips to Europe for young girls were not common in the 1880s, though the wealthy sometimes indulged their offspring if carefully chaperoned. The proposition, when presented, almost caused a breakdown in Mrs. Swift, but the girls were determined.

"Mama, you know women must begin to move about unaccompanied!" Susie would say. "It's just part of their inalienable right. Very soon, we, the women of America, will be speaking out—traveling, teaching, expressing all of our God-given talents—exactly as men do. An oppressive society won't be tolerated much longer."

"Oh, my dears!" Ships, accommodations, strange gentlemen, insidious foreign illnesses. "It simply isn't the thing for American young ladies."

---

3. Another fictitious name.

But they *must* go, the girls insisted. A matter of enormous urgency. Susie's very life might depend on it. It wasn't as if there were no money, and not a penny would be wasted. Why, every cent would be a sound investment for the liberation of womanhood around the world!

Lily, Susie, and Susie's friend, Beth, sailed for England in May of 1884. Their itinerary included two weeks in Ireland, a period in Scotland, a summer in England and winter with friends either in Rome or Naples. The ocean voyage was exhilarating and greatly beneficial to Susie's and Lily's health. Ireland enchanted them and they were euphoric when they reached Glasgow. What a summer it would be! The places, the people, the crystallization of purpose! Women in literature. Women in medicine. Suffragettes on the march in England. Who could tell what mighty conquests would soon be undertaken by women?

On Friday afternoon, as they were being driven in a carriage through Glasgow's downtown streets, reading interesting signs and banners over shops and offices, a completely unfamiliar one caught their attention: SALVATION ARMY.

"Driver, stop!" called the girls, and they jumped out to have a closer look. Whatever could it mean?

SALVATION ARMY
HOLINESS MEETING TONIGHT

"We'll go!" said Susie. "It must be something queer and out of the way."

"Perhaps it might make a magazine article," said Beth, an embryo journalist.

Lily cautioned, "Girls, I don't know about these people except they're really not good form. They've drawn some sharp criticism in the States, and I asked Father about them not long ago. He didn't have first-hand information but said he'd heard them passing under his hotel window in Poughkeepsie, and that's all he cared to know about them."

"Please come, Lily," both girls urged.

"Nothing in this world would induce me to." Lily hoped her decision would deter them, but they went unaccompanied against her wishes. She was waiting up when they returned.

"Lily, the sight of them!" laughed Susie. "The queer bonnets and straight skirts."

"And the scarlet red guernseys on the men. Imagine, for worship!"

"They sing loudly and shout and pray and some of them dance about a bit. They're that happy," said Susie.

"But they are good people," said Beth.

"Yes, I believe in them," nodded Susie.

Lily said no more and thought the matter of The Salvation Army ended, but when the two left dessert uneaten in the hotel next day to attend another meeting, and routed the hotel porter up at 6:30 a.m. on Sunday morning to let them out to go to 7 o'clock prayer meeting, she became anxious and thought, *I shall have to go see for myself.* She recorded her findings when she returned:

"I looked and I listened. A certain pure, good look marked every countenance. These people were no half-crazy fanatics. The calm, holy light in their eyes dispelled forever this illusion. Their speech was rude and unlearned, but it was the outcome of an overwhelmingly personal conviction. They talked of a clean heart and sanctification." And when they said that God had made them good, Lily believed them.

Here at last was the religion for which she longed.

"Sorely, bitterly, against my will, I was forced to believe them," she recorded. "Such lines as I saw in their faces do not grow in a day, nor are they written by a passing emotion. And the evidence of both life lines and eyes 'where shows the heart' corroborated the spoken testimony."

At the conclusion of the service, a sweet-faced woman asked her, "Are you a Christian?"

"No," said Lily directly. "What must I do to be a Christian?"

"Give up your will to God," she replied simply. Lily looked into that pale face and though filled with envy and longing, shook her head.

"I shall never do that, I think."

Next days the girls left Glasgow and toured the Highlands. Then on to Edinburgh.

"We must find The Army," said the younger girls. And they did, with about 600 "evil-faced men and women, representing every state and stage of poverty, vice, and misery," Lily avowed. "Here was embodied before our shocked eyes all the evil of which we had ever heard. Here was sin so apparent in faces, looks, and uttered words as to convince the most skeptical of the need of either a receiving hell or a reclaiming gospel." She asked the Scottish captain, "If I decided to be a Christian, what must I do?"

"Well, first off," he said in broad Scots English, "ye maun repent, give up all your sins, tell Father, go an' ask Him to forgive you an' when ye ask Him that, repentin', ye maun believe that He does it. It's not to believe anythin' more, except as He shows ye. Then ye'll go to work and serve Him wi' all your might. And tha'll be a Christian."

Oh, thought Lily desperately, *the way to Heaven is clear and plain. But what sort of way is it?* She'd better just keep away from The Salvation Army. She would not go again, and when the girls arrived in London, where the Army now had a stronghold, though fiercely persecuted, she refused even to discuss it.

"We've got to find somebody like herself," said Susie, plotting with Beth. At the Army's headquarters on Victoria Street, a young Frenchman was found, brother of an officer, and an intellectual. The girls persuaded Lily to go and converse because they had promised him. Reluctantly and annoyed, she went, meeting him in an empty meeting room in the morning. That he was a gentleman, she immediately observed, but could a gentleman be this disagreeably personal?

"Are you a Christian?" he said almost immediately.

"No," said Lily.

"Then may I tell you how God saved me?"

He concluded his testimony with: "A religion that does not involve entire obedience to God can never be the right kind." And as he spoke she noted that many folk were filing in. A noon-day prayer meeting was about to begin. Lily stood in the midst of the group and told of her search for God. "And now," she said, "I have surrendered my soul to Him and I am determined to serve Him as He shows me how."

And though she meant every word, the fact that one day she would join hands and heart with The Salvation Army never entered her mind. The three girls continued their sightseeing journey but now the question was not, "Which cathedral or museum shall we see?" but "Let's find The Salvation Army!"

They attended 125 meetings in 26 different cities and when the time came to board ship, Lily and Susie decided to stay in London and learn about The Army from the inside. Both had decided to join as laity, notwithstanding their mother's plea to hold off and their father's advice to return home before taking any definite step. Lily knew she had found her place but also that she could never be an officer or do Salvation Army work. She was beyond the age for accepted candidates and was much too frail in health.

Their mother was terrified as each succeeding letter told of their elation. In the United States The Army had not yet begun to recover from the effects of the Moore schism and was in public disrepute, drawing venomous physical and mental abuse. Mrs. Swift wrote repeatedly: "Come home and let Papa talk to you!" and then moaned to Mr. Swift, "Oh, George, fancy our girls consorting with that crowd!"

Mr. Swift discredited much of what he read in the papers regarding the "infamous" Salvation Army, but Mrs. Swift was thoroughly frightened. Ridiculous sketches of Army soldiers, bands, flags, etc. "drove her nearly wild." She wrote the girls, pleading with Lily to come home, but Lily answered with such clear and convincing replies that Mrs. Swift distributed them to various newspapers, who printed them as a counter attack in favor of the Army, in a column titled: "From an American Lady." In these letters, Lily delighted in quoting the spiritual eccentricities of the organization and its founders. After visiting the Booth home she remarked:

I can't make them out. They're either the greatest saints on the face of the earth or the greatest hypocrites. It's as natural to them, children and all, to pray as to eat. Mr. Booth opens a letter at the table, and out drops a ten-pound note for the work. "Look here," he says, "let's get down and thank the Lord for it." And down they all kneel, and have a prayer meeting on the spot.

Regarding suitable clothes to last them over the winter, Lily wrote to her mother:

"You ask how our dresses hold out. Admirably. They are likely to last for 10 years. We wear uniforms, as I told you. For everyday wear we have a skirt and a jersey (navy blue) with SALVATION ARMY embroidered in dark red across the breast. Dress uniform consists of a long princess robe, looped up behind to walking length. I had my uniform very specially made to fit well, to please you. No, my dress doesn't offend any Christians now that I know of. It does offend those who are not Christians, and that is the class I want to get at. If they can't see any outward difference between me and the worldly people, they don't believe in me. If I were to wear fashionable clothing, it is because I love it, and I have no business to love it. And now I don't so why should I wear it? I want to take no thought for my dress. I must, if I follow fashion at all. If I stood up before the roughs with a diamond ring on my hand, and told them how I loved their souls, they'd hoot me. I've got to make them believe that I love them by coming down to their level. When they believe in my love they'll get up to the Lord's level by it.

Of the mission of The Army to the poor, she wrote:

The Army only for roughs? I went this morning to the Salvation Army temple, and sat on the platform, where I could see the audience. It was painfully respectable, old gentlemen with kid gloves, and old ladies all beads, bonnets, and cloaks, young girls with white dresses and feathers. One old gentleman got up and testified it was the Army's *noise* that attracted him—he had no desire or intention to go near them. But when the sound of their band in the street reached him, he wanted to find out what they were making such a row about. He went and got converted and thanked God for the noise!

Her mother asked who preached in the services.

Who preaches? Everybody! There were a hundred sermons last night, and 20 this morning, and they all said something. You don't hear any long spun-out Bible histories, any involved similes, whose ingeniousness makes you forget its object. But you hear Bible truths hurled like bullets. You hear how to get to Heaven, and you see poor dirty wretches start on the way there after the speaking is over.

Lily and Susie were invited to observe The Salvation Army under Emma Booth's direction. This third daughter of the Booths, was at 23, "mother" of the girls' training home for officership. Both girls were soon singing and praying in Emma's meetings, and Lily began to teach special education classes, many of the girls being seriously deprived. She wrote:

I took a class of girls, and was amazed to find what a desire to learn coupled with earnest prayer could do for the dullest mind. . . . I took a class of girls today who had never studied arithmetic before. I put them through the four cardinal rules in one morning. If they weren't well saved, do you suppose I could have done it? No, nor anyone else.

The Swift girls were fascinated by The Army. In spare moments they visited the headquarters on Queen Victoria Street to "get help for our souls," as Lily put it. Here they learned the value of the "common" moment. They went at all hours when it was open and "under all pretexts." Lily evaluated those visits this way:

Whether we loitered in the little front shop looking at photographs and books, went to the top floor to try on a bonnet, dived into the basement for scissors and pamphlets, or even mounted to look over London from the roof, the man or woman in uniform who showed us about was always trying to impart some spiritual gift to us, and slowly, piecemeal it may be, all were helping to get us established in God.

It wasn't long before Susie became editor of The Army's new international magazine, *All the World*. Lily taught cadets, helped with the publication, defended The Army in articles for a local newspaper, and wrote a book regarding the Army's training school entitled, *A Cradle of Empire*. Life was wonderful! Just as she was exulting over it all, she knew a sudden humiliation when, in a rage at Susie for something she felt improper, she realized something interior was still lacking. Because of her usual self-control, no one else knew of her dilemma but she was quite unnerved. What a temper! Waiting like a cobra! That night at meeting someone testified to being saved from evil and consuming temper. Lily went to the penitent-form and asked God to clean her up inside. She went again and again but went away unrewarded.

"Lily, I think you are looking for feeling," a comrade told her. "You must take this gift by faith." She did and at the end of six weeks she suddenly realized she hadn't been angry and hadn't wanted to be. All went well for another few months, then trouble again. She had done nothing, aspired to nothing evil. She had shirked no duty, borne no grudges, had no wild pride or self-seeking. Was she lazy? Physically tired? No. She'd just spent ten days at the seaside. But still that nameless, haunting unrest. Maybe the exuberance couldn't linger.

A friend asked, "Is it well with your soul, Lily?"

"Yes, it must be well, for I am still going on."

"Is it bright in your soul?"

"Well," said Lily. Then she told of her difficulty.

"Do you read your Bible?" asked the officer.

"Of course I do."

"How much and how and when?"

"Well . . ." Lily confessed that sometimes she was very busy, or too tired or sleepy, and sometimes crowded the reading out altogether. "But it's the Lord's work that is responsible, you know. Not my own pleasure."

"It's easy to see where your trouble is," the officer said. "Now, will you promise me to spend an hour every day in prayer and Bible study?"

"An hour?" she gasped. "Why, I couldn't! I haven't the time! You have no idea how rushed I am."

"I do know. We all are. You've got to make time. Cut out something else." He argued and pleaded until she promised to "try it for a month." This was the turning point in Lily's career. The necessity for feeding the spirit was never again forgotten. That we must hunger and thirst after righteousness and then eat what God provides she never again doubted. In May of 1885 Lily and Susie returned to America, Susie for a brief visit before returning to her editorship of *All the World* in the autumn, and Lily to begin meetings in her own locale. Their father had suffered grave business reverses through ill-advised investments, but it made no difference to the girls.

"Never mind, darlings. We've got each other and that's the main thing, and we can certainly live off the farm," was Lily's comment.

"Well," said Mr. Swift, "if you look at it that way, it will be all right."

Friends and family did not know what to make of the Swift sisters. Such lovely girls and hadn't they always had everything and been impeccably reared? Faithful church-goers, too! Surely they knew how they were disgracing their parents. There were no deprived or sinful folk in Amenia anyhow. The girls knew different, and so did old Aunt Sarah. "Law," said she, "as much plumb wickedness in this place as any Londontown. You jus' don' know."

It was a summer of victorious salvation work. Meetings were held initially in the Methodist church. People came and filled the altar rail after the "new religion" was preached. So great was the interest in the meetings that they had to be continued during the week in the village hall. Then came the riff-raff. Drunkards, wife beaters, opium eaters, the violently vicious of both sexes. Sarah's 16-year-old son was converted, later becoming a minister. At first all nearby churches welcomed Lily's preaching. There were so many young men who "forsook idle and evil ways" that Lily rented a reading room where they could meet to read, talk, and play games. Autumn came and Susie went back to England. Lily worked on, prayed, visited, and now emphasized in her preaching a spiritual experience of life-dedication that began to cause criticism. Villagers turned away, church doors were closed to her one by one and though her parents gave active support, she soon found herself without a place to preach but with a growing congregation of the very poor and very ex-sinful. This is a sample of the kind of preaching she presented:

You say you want power but you can't overcome? And that God's law seems too difficult? If that be true, it proves that the soul is out of order. Go to the Physician . . . the law of God, written in the hearts of His people, becomes part of their inmost being, and it works out in their conduct as naturally as their physical life does in the exercise of the different parts of the body. It is not difficult for a healthy eye to show us pictures of our surroundings; not unpleasant for a healthy ear to report to us the sounds of nature; nor is it either hard or distasteful for a healthy soul to carry out the whole will of God, to latch every detail of conduct to His perfect law. Difficulty and pain do not attend natural workings; they indicate an unhealthy or diseased state.

Dear friend, you do not need power but peace! And that is what is promised. Jesus said: "Peace I leave with you. My peace I give unto you." *That* is your legacy. Have you secured it? You would not hesitate to secure a gift of dollars or diamonds which was yours by bequest. It is not a little thing God has willed for you: "Peace like a river," enriching and making fruitful all the land where you dwell. "Peace which passeth all understanding."

It will keep your soul strong under trials that seem inexplicable. And when the demons seem to let loose upon the soul, and the waves rise mountains high, even then this peace remains unbroken.

Oh, don't pray for power to overcome or to do anything else! We are not to seek power but the Empowerer. God has no power to let, like the property owners' long rivers and waterside. It was never known that He gave His power away. But He comes in Himself to the surrendered, believing human heart, and abiding there, exerts His power in us and through us. The command is not "seek ye power," but "seek ye ME."

Pray instead that God will cleanse His temple and abide in it forever. Then when you believe His promise in this very thing, it will be done. His glory will fill your temple, and you will not be able at times to distinguish His presence there from His presence in the greater, higher Heaven where you used to think He alone dwelt.

When the Holy Spirit comes to abide in you, you will receive power to witness unto Jesus wherever you may be. Jesus told His disciples that when the Comforter came, He would testify of Jesus, and he repeated it just before He ascended into Heaven. Over and over again we are told that for us Jesus is the Possessor of Divine power. His indwelling alone constitutes our power.

Of this period, she wrote,

A combined effort is being made by the churches here to break up my work by driving me out of the Methodist church building and the village hall. Though I can control the church situation and could build a new hall, yet the Lord does not lead me to do either. My heart aches, but bless the dear Lord! Never a soul comes here to stay but He gives it to me!

Her own experience grew stronger and stronger, and her appreciation of Divine guidance increased. Once, an old-time acquaintance remarked, "Lily, do you really believe all those miracles actually happened?"

"You mean," said Lily, "for example, Elisha's making the axe-head swim? Yes, I believe it. Why not? That was merely the overcoming for a moment of a law of nature; but God used a man full of His Spirit to win my will over to His side and so he overcame the law of sin in my heart. I *know* that. And isn't it easy after that to believe that God can do anything?"

"Yes," said the friend. "The change in you *is* a miracle. When I remember your training, your heredity, your habits, associations, tastes, and see you now as totally changed as if you were recreated, I am bound to believe in miracles."

Soon Lily's fame as a woman preacher had spread and she was invited to Boston to speak to an interested though somewhat critical audience—critical both of a woman preacher and of an experience that guaranteed inner peace.

She stood before this group proclaiming the Kingdom of God and a conquering Christ when a tall, gaunt seminarian strode in and, seating himself quietly, became fascinated with both the message and the messenger.

APPENDIX

Ancestry

The Swift family's sojourn in the United States dates back to colonial days when William Swift came to America from England in the famed "Boston Immigration" of 1630-1. William Swift Jr. was born in England, spent his life in the United States and died in January of 1706. Succeeding generations include:

William Swift Jr.	b. England	d. 1706
Jiveh	b. 1665	d. 1794
Jabez	b. 1700	d. 1767
Elisha Swift	b. 1731	
General John Swift	b. Kent, Eng. 1761	d. July 14, 1814

General Swift immigrated to the United States in his youth, served in the revolutionary army, was made Brigadier General of New York troops in March of 1812, was shot at or near Fort George, Niagara River, and died from the effects on July 14, 1814. He was the grandfather of Elizabeth Swift Brengle.

Lily's Favorite Quotations

In Lily's earliest books, chapters are headed with favorite quotations. Here are some of them:

Now I confess, I look upon religion as a kind of diet, which can only be when I make a constant practice of it, when throughout the whole twelve months, I ne'er lose sight of it.—Goethe

As my days go on I am less and less particular as to ecclesiasticism, and more and more profoundly impressed with the thought that the exponent of true religion is not to be found in creeds nor books, nor ecclesiastical bodies, but in the living souls of holy men.—Henry Ward Beecher

It is never too late to give up our prejudices. No way of thinking or doing, however ancient, can be trusted without proof.—David Thoreau

To saturate life with God, and the world with Heaven, that is the genius of Christianity.—Robertson

The greatest of all the mysteries of life and the most terrible, is the corruption of even the sincerest religion which is not founded on rational, effective, humble and helpful action.—Ruskin

> Children small,
> Spilt like blots about the city.
> Wicked children, with peaked chins,
> And old foreheads! There are many
> With no pleasure except sins,
> Gambling with a stolen penny.
> —Elizabeth Barrett Browning

When Christ divests Himself of His hat and boots He will conquer India!—Keshub Chunder Sen

Your favorite piano has scarcely done so much as the poor despised drum to help Christ to win back His own. . . .—Smith

There are, it may be, so many kinds of voices in the world and none of them is without signification.—Paul

We are much bound to them that do succeed; but in a more pathetic sense are bound to such as fail.—Ingelow

Let no soldier fly. He that is truly dedicated to war hath no self love.—Shakespeare

You hear many outcries against sensation; but I can tell you it is not less sensation that we want, but more.—Ruskin

Not struck enough to overturn our faith, but shake it—make us learn . . . how hard it is to be a Christian growing.—Anon

> Then forth I went,
> Forsaking father, mother, all I had
> And all I hoped for through the sunny years,
> Content forevermore to follow Him
> Who thus had summoned me. In weariness,
> In painfulness, in perils by the way,
> Through awful vigils in the wilderness,
> Through storms of trouble, hatred, and reproach,
> I followed Him. . . .

—B.M.

Aunt Sarah's Drop Cookies

The following recipe is as close as we can come to Aunt Sarah's recipe for her famous drop cookies, as Elizabeth remembers them. They are especially delicious put together in twos with pink-tinted confectioner's sugar frosting.

½ C butter	1½ t baking powder
¾ C sugar	½ t salt
2 eggs	2 T lemon juice
1¾ C flour	2 T water

Cream butter and sugar. Add eggs and beat. Add sifted dry ingredients alternately with juice and water. Drop from tsp on greased sheet. Mod. oven—375 deg., 8–10 min.

One of Lily's Favorite Poems

Call of the Drum

> All faint and far away I hear
> The calling of the drum
> Its rhythmic thrumming, drawing near,
> Is ever pleading, "Come!"
> The colors are waving

My heart throbs with craving—
As nearer
And clearer,
And louder,
And prouder,
Its melody grows, as the sound comes and goes,
"Come! Come!"
Is the call of the drum

Now bright and grand and near at hand,
I hear the calling drum.
The flag, by gallant breezes fanned,
Is beckoning, "Oh, come!"
We'll rush to the clamour
Of strife, with its glamor,
And swelling,
And telling,
The story
Of glory
The drum sings in glee as it passes by me,
"Come! Come!"
Is the song of the drum.

All faint and far away I hear
The ever-calling drum;
Now singing low, now singing clear,
In its insistent "Come!"
With tones sweet and hollow,
It lures me to follow,
Far away,
Through the day,
It calls me,
Enthralls me—
The lilt of its beating my heart is repeating,
"Come! Come!"
Is the call of the drum.

—Anon

Three

Sam and Lily Brengle

When Sam Brengle took his first look at delicate little Lily Swift preaching in a Boston church, he was captured. The bright light of love shone on her slender features. She was earnest. She was humorous. She was knowledgeable. She was eloquent. A gamin angel. Still, he had no way of guessing when he had prayed, "Lord, choose a wife for me," that the Almighty would act so promptly and that their marriage would be acknowledged by many as not only God-oriented but also God-ordained—despite every reason for conflict and unhappiness that many marriages cannot survive: long separations, physical frailty of wife, prolonged illness and inactivity of husband, frail children with lingering illnesses and disease, insufficient finance and few friends during early family crises.

True, Sam had long imagined such a woman as Lily and had, to the best of his ability, prepared himself for her and for marriage. He recounted:

> One of the guards of my adolescent years, during those lonely periods after Mother died, was the thought of a wife to whom one day I wanted to give myself as pure and unsoiled as I hoped to find her. When tempted to run after forbidden pleasures, that thought was one of the great restraints

of my life—one of the supreme protective influences. I wanted so to live
that I could open my heart and tell my wife my whole life without
shame.

Sam had an exalted opinion of womanhood, and measured his
dream by the best he had heard and imagined. He longed for that
woman:

I came to feel that part of my mission in life, one of the objects of my being,
was to make some one little woman happy, while to injure a woman, to
mar her life and blast her happiness, seemed to me—and still seems—the
supreme cursedness and treason against the most sacred rights and claims
of humanity. From Mother I unconsciously got a high ideal of gentle
sweetness, purity and all other womanly virtues which adorn a home and
make it a haven of rest and a center of inspiration, courage, and noble
ambition.

Now, listening to this daring little woman, he was overcome.
"I lost my heart," he said later. "Here she was, the sweet, gracious, cultured woman, filled with God's love, one my head and
heart approved, and for whose sake I had denied myself in lonely
hours of fierce temptation, and for whom I had prayed and watched
and waited."

Now what? He couldn't bring himself to converse with her. There
had to be a correct first step. The next morning he wrote her a
letter and began a correspondence which never ended "till her tired
little hand laid down the pen forever."

Sam knew better than to blurt out his love and wrote about only
spiritual matters, though he did not hesitate to let her know they
shared much truth and had a singularly similar regard for and
attitude toward life. Lily was appreciative of "the sanctified interest
of a brother in Christ," and not long after she returned to Amenia,
invited him to conduct a revival campaign in the church where
through Salvation Army methods the membership had been
doubled in a few months. Because Banker Swift's house was the
place where preachers were entertained, Sam spent many hours

with Lily while there, discussing spiritual matters and "poking about the village, Army fashion."

In many respects the two were strikingly alike: in their sensitivity, appreciation of and adeptness with words, acceptance of persons unlike themselves, and in forthright honesty. Even during this initial meeting, with Sam madly in love with Lily, he felt compelled to inform her of certain observations concerning her spiritual life. There was a serious lack, he believed:

She worked the limit, and she prayed fervently, but seemed to me to lack appropriating faith—the faith that takes, receives, and is glad; the faith which rests as it works; the faith that drives the wrinkles from the brow, the burden off the heart, leaving the face sunny and the heart free; the faith that makes every prayer end in a burst of thanksgiving and which lingers with the Lord for sweet fellowship and communion when prayer is done.

He pointed this out to her in a spirit of tender frankness that would forever characterize their companionship. They talked and wrote about this lack, but the light did not come to Lily for some weeks, not until, due to unceasing activity, she was obliged to go to a sanatorium (Victorian rest resort) to avoid a complete breakdown. There certainly was something missing, she knew that. She prayed, "Lord, there's something I haven't got. Show it to me." Immediately, two words bounced into her mind:

MORE ABUNDANTLY

More abundantly? *Scripture*. What was the remainder of that quotation? She hastily consulted her Bible. More abundantly. More abundantly. There! Words of Jesus. Jesus speaking:

I AM COME THAT THEY MIGHT HAVE LIFE, AND THAT THEY MIGHT HAVE IT MORE ABUNDANTLY.

Of course!
She wrote Sam:

Samuel Logan Brengle
at age twenty-three

Elizabeth (Lily) Swift
in her early twenties.

"Sisterly Kindness,"
from "The War Cry,"
April 13, 1895.

Brigadier-General John Swift,
leader in the Revolutionary War of 1812,
and ancestor of Elizabeth Swift Brengle.

Lily, prior to her
marriage to Sam.

"Ruffians Attack,"
from "The War Cry,"

Lily's Father,
George H. Swift

Brengle's daughter,
Elizabeth, age six.

Elizabeth Brengle Reed

Oh, Sam, you *have* helped me. You helped me when you showed me that Jesus wanted me for something more than a servant. I had never looked any higher. But I rose higher, and it was through you I did so, by keeping my promises to you of praying more in the way of communion and waiting on God. Sam, I feel his love about me like sunshine all the while.

Ever since He gave me life more abundantly I have forgotten more and more my servantship though that was sweet and dear to me—and have come into the higher life of a friend.

The idea that He could love me so, that He would care for my fellowship and communion, and I should share this with Him, was so tremendous! It is still, and fills me with wonder, love, and praise.

For months they corresponded, sharing insights, information, platform techniques. Then, during autumn of 1886 Lily prepared for another trip to England in order to write a projected book on the experiences of new Salvation Army converts. Sam decided to ask the momentous question.

"Lily, I love you! Please marry me."

"Oh, Sam, no!" Lily was genuinely surprised at the offer and burdened that now their friendship would have to end. She wrote a little later: "Your proposal has filled me with joy and with intense sadness. I feel that your love, if I could be your wife, would be the crown of my womanhood. But it cannot be." She then listed some of the reasons: her health was extremely delicate; her father had suffered financial reverses and she didn't want to leave him; and she was 11 years older than he. They would be poor and in time Sam would have a "broken down old woman" on his hands.

Sam paid no attention whatsoever to her plea to forget her: "You are surely under a spell, an illusion! All my sanctified commonsense says loudly and clearly, 'You must not marry him.' Some day you will be glad that I couldn't think as you did, and that I kept you free. I am sure that God means better things for you. Please ask Him, as I do, to set you free."

She then generously mentioned two others, with either of whom, she decided, Sam would be much happier than with her. At her request, he met them and found both lovely. But compared with Lily they were "as water unto wine," and he went on begging.

One day Lily gave him a little book without a by-line. He read it with deepest interest, not suspecting that she was its author. Entitled *A Cradle of Empire,* it dealt with Salvation Army Cadet training. On another day while they rode in the Swift carriage among the beautiful hills near her home, she mentioned an illegitimate baby, whose mother had so mistreated it that Lily had taken it home and kept it for months, nursing it back to health. As she described the baby, Sam imagined her delight with children of her own, as one who viewed motherhood with "great and solemn joy."

Still another time as they stood around the family piano in Amenia, Lily slipped out into a hallway, and Sam felt bereft:

My eyes followed her, and my whole heart went out after her. I did not want to die for her but to live for her. I wanted to put my arms about her, to comfort her, provide for her, protect her, bear her burdens, be her shield and receive every blow of adversity or sorrow or misfortune that might befall her. I no longer thought of what she might bring or give to me, but only of what I might give to and suffer for her. Without realizing it, I had entered the world of sacrificial love and utter devotion.

Sam went right on expressing his love. The time for her to board ship was at hand when she wrote:

You should not waste your life. And what about my own soul? "A married woman careth for the things of this world, and that she may please her husband" (I Corinthians 7:34). I am sure that I should get worldly and be always thinking how to look young and as nearly pretty as I could, just to please you. I should surely in that way put you before God, and I dare not risk that.

You say that our life must be one of utter devotion to the Man Christ Jesus? How that fills my soul with joy. I am so glad for you. I rejoice in you. *I cannot ever risk hindering that.* I do trust Him for you.

And off she sailed to write her books: *What Hinders You?* and *Drum Taps.*

Drum Taps required much first-hand investigation so there was little time to think of Sam. She was eager to present her findings in colloquial speech, no easy task. The book is a treasury of the speech and mores of the period. Her literary style is perceptive, economical, and descriptive, her taste impeccable. She exhibits a lively, sharp vocabulary and her sense of unity is appealing. Lily Swift was a competent literary writer of her period. In introductory remarks concerning the first voyage across the Atlantic, she recalled:

And when we left the barracks we had no more individual like for Salvation Army methods than we brought there. But we recognized that there were folks who did like these methods—people, who, but for The Army, would still be spending this Sabbath night in public houses or gambling halls; people who through it had come in contact with the Gospel and been humanized and converted. And in view of these results, we reverently recognized even the tumultuous, jarring drum as the messenger of God.

Her first impressions of Salvation Army congregations were graphically presented, sometimes poetically:

> Faces! Oh my God
> we call those faces?
> Men's and women's
> and children's faces?
> Phew!
> We'll call them vices, festering to despair,,
> or sorrows petrifying to vices;
> not a finger touch of God
> left whole on them.

Of unorthodox Salvation Army methods Lily commented:

What's the use of telling people to come to church when they know of no rational reasons why they should? And when, if they go, they find themselves among people using forms of words which have never been explained to them, ceremonies performed which to them are entirely without meaning, sermons preached which, as often as not, have no meaning or when they have, a meaning intelligible only to those who have studied religion all their lives?

She observed that she felt the necessity of "radical measures to catch people as never before and really longed for a bass drum and a cornet to stir them up and draw them in."

Lily admitted the vulgarity of flaming circus bills announcing services, a method often used by early-day Salvationists, but maintained their compelling value in reaching the outcast, many of whom would not otherwise enter a place of worship. ". . . when former friends and acquaintances of a man who used to worry live rats to death with his teeth, or the one who ate dead cats on a wager, see these individuals announced to speak publicly in a Salvation Army barracks, they will walk 20 miles to hear him."

Her style grew stronger, more forthright as the book progressed:

Society has been, for years, trying to elevate the masses by the leverage of Christianity, but ignoring, for the most part, the simple and fundamental truth that a lever must go under the mass to be raised. The Salvation Army has been raised from the under-stratum of society by the leverage of a Christianity which came down to it, and now, in turn, it has hold of the lever. It only asks a place whereon to stand, to *move the world.*

That was the conclusion of *Drum Taps* and of Elizabeth Swift, an American lady, in 1886.

Lily espoused women's rights as few dared to in that day: "Surely," she wrote, "surely, though very slowly the time is coming to be civilized if not Christianized to the point of helping instead of hindering even 'those women which labor in the Gospel,' and to recognize all rights which God does not deny:

> The rights of woman—what are they?
> The right to labor and to pray;
> The right to lead the soul to God,
> Along the path her Saviour trod.

She further declared, quoting Isaiah: "Rise up, ye women that are at ease; hear my voice, ye careless daughters! . . . The Lord gave the word; great was the company of women that published it" (Isaiah). And one of her favorites was a quotation from Gurney: "We will know that there are no women among us more generally distinguished for modesty, gentleness, order, and right submission to their brethren than those who have been called by their Divine Master unto the exercise of the Christian ministry." She spurred on sister Salvationists by reminding them of an early-day poem by an officer comrade, T. C. Marshall:

> Dear Saviour, I am Thine,
> Thou hast commissioned me,
> And it is now chief joy of mine,
> Thy soldier girl to be.
>
> Dear Saviour, Thou art mine!
> With Thee I fear no foe;
> Through earth to Heaven,
>   my hand in Thine,
> Thy soldier girl I'll go.

Lily was deeply impressed with the fervor and sacrificial spirit of many Salvationists then being brutally mistreated. She published this poem in *All the World* on February 4, 1886. It told of Louis Jeanmonod, who was murdered for his belief.

> Just a Swiss lad, sturdy and tall,
> Keeping the door of Quai Valmy hall,
> Working for God in the dark, that was all—
>   Jeanmonod!
>
> Bound for "the field," with the morrow's sun,
> Days of soldierly training done,
> Pledged to fight till the battle is won,
>   Glad to go.

Struck down there by the riotous crowd,
Tranquilly meeting its curses loud,
Just inside while his comrades bowed
    Low in prayer.

Not a murmur from Jeanmonod.
"Comrade, that was a fearful blow,"
All he said when it laid him low,
    Done to death.

Battling with pain instead of sin,
First of our rank with the martyrs to win,
Stephen and Zwingli have welcomed him in—
    Jeanmonod!

Lily's story of Larry the drummer is altogether enchanting, exhibiting a grasp of substance over signature, truth over tag, nature over name, and of the acceptance of experiential discovery of the Divine Presence. When Lily met Larry he was the faithful uniformed drummer in an English corps. Through his ministry hundreds of people had been converted, appreciative of his simple tactics. As one of them expressed it: "We be main thick-headed here, but Larry he talked so simple—like a child could understand him. And *he do live it.*"

Larry had entered Her Majesty's service when 12, and it wasn't long before he became a "prime drunk and fighter," filthy as they come. He'd been kicked from the door of The Salvation Army by the burly doorkeeper many times, and when finally he got into the gallery in order "to see the show," he was faintly disappointed. Look there, chum! A few plain people sitting on a platform, talking about Heaven. Drivel, all this chatter. Like a foreign language. But the singing! Ah, the singing he could enjoy. The clapping and the singing. Sometimes they sang a song over and over and then he got the hang of it. And he liked their looks. They looked so pure—and so clean. So nice and clean.

Larry described the meeting to Lily:

They got up and said God had made 'em good and happy, and I made up my mind to be like 'em. I knew nothing of Christ but I wanted to be changed like my mates. I asked some sinners sitting near me what you must do to be like them on the platform. They told me those had got saved, and I asked what that were. They said it were to lead a better life, and if I was tired of the life I wor leading I could change the same as those, by going out to the penitent-form and praying. "Pray," I say. "What's that?"

The "sinners" began to laugh and would tell poor Larry no more. At the proper time Larry went out to pray nonetheless. Knowing his background and thinking him "shamming," no one knelt beside him to help. When the Captain asked all who were "saved" to stand, the rest stood, but not Larry. He kept kneeling till the meeting was closed. Then he got up and sat on a bench, but still no one bothered with him. However, in Larry's words, "Everything wor different. I went on outside the barracks and I felt different and I couldn't tell what wor the matter with me. I didn't know who God wor, nor at Christ had died, but I knew I wor changed."

And so did everyone else in Larry's life know he was changed. He passed right by the public house; his old drunken mother asked "what wor the matter" with him, and his factory mates all questioned.

"But I couldn't tell them," said Larry, "for I didn't know what to call it. Next day all over the shop the news went that I'd joined The Salvation Army. They cursed and they coaxed but I never spoke. Nearly five weeks I had nothing to say."

Larry couldn't "make out how to pray" but he never missed a night at the Army hall and always sat by himself. One night he asked some nearby "sinners," "who Jesus Christ wor," but only laughter was the response. He watched people and listened and "got hold of" the cry of "Lord, help me!" for a prayer. His mother threatened him with a poker and locked him out, his mates tempted and taunted him but "Lord, help me!" always worked. Larry noticed that Salvationists carried Bibles, so he bought one and learned to read from the Army songbook. One night the Captain called on Larry to pray.

"What shall I say?" asked Larry.

"Ask the Lord," said the Captain. And he did. Then a "special" (visiting minister) visited the corps and Larry asked him what "saved" meant. The officer questioned him for 20 minutes and announced that Larry was indeed "saved." Saved was to be changed then—to care no more for the drink, or bad language, or fighting, and to love all "that wor good in people," to mind the things of God and want always to be better still." And after that he came to know the name of Jesus.

A strange story but one that Lily would feel compelled to ponder, appreciate, and record. Her books completed, Lily sailed for home. Sam was waiting, for though busy in her absence with much travel, new opportunities to preach, he was even more certain that Lily was the "little woman" God had chosen for him.

Interestingly, it was one of Lily's books, a short volume concerning Salvation Army cadet training entitled *A Cradle of Empire,* that prodded him to the decision not only to become a member of The Salvation Army but an officer. "This little book," he said later, "finally tipped the scales and dropped me into The Army. I was a student in the theological school of Boston University, and the apostolic simplicity and spirit and devotion of the Army's school was so different from the scholastic spirit of the theological school that it broke my heart. Bursting into tears, I cried out, 'These are my people!'"

"Lily," said Sam, as before, "I love you. Please marry me."

They began to laugh.

"Very well, Sam," said Lily. "I shall."

The wedding was planned. It must be simple; of course, they would both be dressed in uniform. And it must glorify God. Sam bought a plain gold ring and had inscribed in it: *Holiness Unto The*

Lord.[1] This would be their secret. This would be their sign. This would be their security. Later, Sam explained, "We covenanted to watch over each other jealously, each helping the other to keep in the experience of that moment. We testified, we preached, we wrote in season, out of season, that God might be glorified in the hearts and lives of His people. We prayed together and apart for this."

And now the wedding. They had decided that, immediately after the wedding, Sam would sail to the Salvation Army's international "training home" in London. For Sam, this was necessary, for though William Booth might possibly waive the training period in the light of Sam's qualifications, Sam knew little of Army methods. Lily would wait and prepare herself at home for the great co-ministry ahead.

"Why, I never heard of such a thing!" gasped Mrs. Swift.

"Neither did I," responded Lily placidly.

Many acquaintances did not understand at all—or try to. What kind of arrangement was this? Why not wait under such circumstances? Or why not accompany Sam? With all his education, he certainly didn't need what The Salvation Army could offer.

The wedding was performed in the Swift parlor (as was often the custom in the 1880s) on May 19, 1887. The beautiful Victorian home was decorated with flowers from the Swift garden; tables were laden with food from the Swift kitchen for the overflow crowd which attended. Invited, of course, were the local aristocracy and, even more naturally, Lily's converts—the poor of the township: attendants at Lily's meetings, farm hands, kitchen girls, and Aunt Sarah's family and friends. After the ceremony, as was Salvation Army custom, both Sam and Lily testified to what the love of God meant in their lives and how He had brought them together, blessed them and now promised to be with them "till death did them part."

They had a few days' honeymoon and then off sailed Sam. Arriving in London, he was interviewed by General William Booth.

---

1. *Holiness unto the Lord* is still the inscription used on the cloth of the holiness table in every Salvation Army hall.

It was June 1, of 1887, when the hawk-eyed patriarch surveyed 27-year-old Samuel Logan Brengle and brusquely declared: "Brengle, you belong to the dangerous classes. You have been your own boss for so long that I don't think you will want to submit to Salvation Army discipline. We are an army, and we demand obedience."

"Well, General," said Sam matter-of-factly, "I have received the Holy Spirit as my Sanctifier and Guide. I feel He has led me to offer myself to you. Give me a chance."

Sam was sent to join 17 other young men in the London training home and immediately was apprised of some of his shortcomings and inabilities:

1. His pride was tested: he was assigned for a period to black the boots of other cadets. He resisted inwardly. It seemed such a waste of time. "Lord," he prayed, "am I burying my talent? Is this the best they can do for me in The Salvation Army? Am I a fool? Have I followed my own fancy 3,000 miles to black boots?" Then he remembered that Jesus had washed young men's feet, and he rubbed all the harder.

2. His scholarly and "long-winded" sermons were quite unacceptable and he wrote Elizabeth that he was "to spend some time with the Booths and others, who are to take me in hand and train me to be brief and 'Blood and Fire'!"

3. He lacked business training and organizational ability, considered important to the on-going march of The Army. He wrote Lily: ". . . If I had business qualifications, they'd make a D.C. (divisional commander) of me at once, but not considering that expedient, they are waiting to find a place for me. Well, inasmuch as I am not a businessman . . . I'm going to draw comfort from Acts 7:24. I know God has a place for me. I think He saw that I would be in The Salvation Army and it is highly probable that He had somewhat to do with my training for the work."

Sam's single passion was heart cleanness and Christlikeness—for himself, for Lily, for The Army, "for the whole world of professed followers of the holy Son of God."

Now that Lily had given Sam her heart, and they were wed, her childlikeness and delight in their union flowered into her letters. With no embarrassment she wrote:

> Oh, my dear Sam, I am so glad I have got you! It doesn't seem like having you exactly, at 3,500 miles distance, but I've been reading over some of your letters and besides other things, they have given me a delightful sense of ownership. Love, my love, you are mine in Christ Jesus, our Lord, and distance can't affect that blessed fact . . . and so I delight in you this morning. He *did* keep me for you, my darling, though I can't think much of your gain in it, and I'm so glad. . . .

That the love expressed in their correspondence would last forever, they were sure. But that for a lifetime, more often than not, it would have to be exhibited in correspondence, they could never guess, and perhaps would have doubted their own courage to sustain it, had they known. There is an old saying: "He tempers the wind to the shorn lamb." In the lives of Sam and Lily Brengle the converse may be true: "He strengthens the lamb for the wildest wind."

Sam's homecoming was felicity itself. Hallelujah! Hallelujah! Hallelujah! Very soon they discovered just how mobile and adaptive their hallelujahs would have to be. In the first nine months of their officership, from December, 1887, to September, 1888, Sam commanded three corps, short appointments being customary at that time: Taunton, Massachusetts; and South Manchester and Danbury, Connecticut. "One worst, one best, and one in between," he described them. After the first three months of getting established, Lily joined him, now pregnant with their first child, writing just before she left home:

"I shall be home on Monday. I can't wait another day. My heart calls out for you so, darling, darling. I am coming home! Home! You are my home, do you know it? Do you realize it? My love, *you are all my world.*"

To them their world was beautiful because of this, though they knew poverty, shabby quarters, overwork. Not long after their reunion, however, Lily became very ill in Danbury and returned to Amenia for treatment, the pioneer Army offering few aids to the ill or injured. At the moment of her leavetaking "a long line of trials" began for Sam.

Only months before, Danbury had been known as one of the Army's strongholds, despite the fact that The Army in the United States had not yet overcome completely the Moore scandal that had almost caused its dissolution. Both Marshall Ballington and General William Booth had recently visited the corps which had opened in November of 1885 and which rejoiced in a large soldiery, as many as 60 soldiers often marching to open-air services which were enhanced by a competent brass band tutored by George E. Ives, father of the famed American musician Charles Ives. When permitted, the band paraded to the accompaniment of a boom bass drum and frequently presented extremely popular "musical festivals."[2]

Concurrently, however, appeared the evils of persecution by authorities who more often than not withheld permission to play in the streets;[3] persecution from "toughs" who vocally and physically beset them;[4] and the distress of having the American Salvation Army (Moore's group) open in the same city,[5] and the competitive

---

2. *News Times,* July 15, 1887: "The musicale of The Salvation Army was fairly attended, the success was such as to encourage the army to repeat these novel exercises."

3. *News Times,* July 14, 1887: "The Salvation Army has applied for permission to again parade through streets, using their musical instruments, and were refused."

4. *News Times,* Sept. 8, 1887: "Two or three drunken loafers did their best to break up the meeting of the Salvation Army last evening. . . . They procured two small dogs and throwing them into the ring, tried to get them to fight . . . then took the animals in their arms so that they could scratch the necks of the Army women. . . . As the Army started away, the roughs pushed them around and one of them was knocked down . . . language too vile to be listened to."

5. *News Times,* Nov. 11, 1886: "An American Independence corps, is to be started next week. A soldiers' meeting will be held on Saturday night, and already 25 soldiers have enlisted in the new corps. It is the intention of this company to run a

Christian Temperance Union organized by a dissenting pocket of soldiers.

Several times before Sam's arrival, The Army had been without a home base because the rent could not be raised, and more than once without officer leadership. At such times, soldiers directed operations, one of these being George Washington, a "trophy of grace" who had escaped slavery, had been imprisoned for six years as a receiver of stolen goods, and had eventually capitulated in a striking manner to God—and The Salvation Army. By the time Sam arrived in Danbury, George was mentioned in a local newspaper as "the famed Salvationist."

During one arrest just before Sam's tenure, the *News Times* reported that Salvationists were taken into custody "while prayer was being offered by George Washington"; and on February 27, 1888, reported that after an assault on George by a streetcar employee that ended in George's being forced from the car, he was "abused both with tongue and fists." The report concluded: "No resistance nor complaint was made but several of the passengers announced their willingness to appear against the assailant if George would but report him."[6]

Immediately preceding Sam's appointment serious "scandal" had appeared in the work, possibly a combination of onslaughts. At any rate, only 13 soldiers remained, two of whom Sam remembered vividly in later years—a little hunchback girl "about 3'6'" and "a big black man named George Washington who was about 6'3'." With these two and a lame lieutenant whose "leg dragged behind him," Sam marched the streets singing, "We are the Army that shall conquer!" and "We are marching on to war—we are, we are, we are!"

---

newspaper of their own in town, and to have a regular organized band. They will elect a captain of their own when further organized."

6. See Chapter III, Appendix, p. 113 for sketch of the life of George Washington.

His corps was housed in a very old barnlike hall but was soon ousted by an unfriendly landlord; there was grave financial difficulty—no salary, and payments for rent of the quarters were long overdue. He made some converts but neither they nor most of the few others met Sam's high standards for Salvationists, and he was heartbroken over their petty jealousy and envyings.

"I was so new to the Army and so unacquainted with the class of people with whom I was laboring that I don't think I was considered a very successful Captain," recalled Sam, "but I did preach the Word with love and many tears."

Open ridicule grew; ruffians tempted, taunted, and terrorized, the Salvationists and police did nothing to dissuade them. Especially harassing were their attacks with firecrackers during the summer, hurled into the open-air ring. Sam also fell ill with malaria.

One night, tramping through the muddy streets with George Washington, the little hunchback girl, and his lame lieutenant, he was accosted by the insidious whisper of an inner voice as they passed an imposed Methodist church. *"You are a fool!"* the voice said. *"If you had remained in the church, you might have been pastor of this church with a congregation of hundreds of members; but you fool, you are a pastor only of this big negro and this little hunchback girl!"*

Sam felt he did not underestimate the value of his trusted helpers but did feel that God might be condemning him for wasting his talents, for being "a wicked and slothful servant." He was tempted. *"Why, Lord? I gave You my all. Is this proper? Is it necessary?"* A fierce spiritual battle ensued. March on . . . give up! March on . . . give up! Determined not to sulk or indulge himself in self-pity he marched on and back at the quarters got out his Bible. In *Timothy* he read Paul's words: "I suffer as an evildoer even unto bonds, but the Word of God is not bound." Liberty! The last phrase burst upon his spirit like lightning, freed him into everlasting light—a newer, more powerful freedom than he had hitherto known even on the day of his heart's cleansing.

He saw Paul in prison "eager to get out and evangelize the world and shepherd his converts, but instead he was in prison chained to a Roman soldier. But he won the soldier and other soldiers to Jesus until there were saints in Caesar's household." Sam said to himself, *"The Army may put me into the darkest little corner it has, but by the grace of God, I will preach the Word until it reaches around the world, for the Word of God is not bound!"* Many years later he said of this experience: "God gave me one of the greatest victories of my life. . . . He liberated my spirit and made me free as a bird in the midst of the cramping circumstances in which I was then living and working." He wrote Lily: "I'm like a thirsty Arab following mirages. My hopes are suddenly lifted high and then dashed to the ground. But glory to God! My faith holds like an anchor. His grace is sufficient."

After three and one-half months in Danbury, he again received marching orders. By this time Lily had joined him. He read:

YOU ARE APPOINTED AS OFFICER IN CHARGE OF BOSTON NUMBER 1 CORPS. PROCEED AT ONCE.

Boston!

"Boston, Sam?"

"Darling, I have no appetite," said Sam and left the table. The condition of the city, so far as The Salvation Army was concerned, was disastrous. A little later, Major Brewer, a divisional officer, described it thus: "The only thing to find fault with in this beautiful, cultured city is its sin. There are nearly a thousand licensed saloons (population 450,000 in 1890), hundreds of brothels and, some say, 10,000 fallen women. Here, amid all our wealth, culture and learning, are heard the snap of the revolver, the dash of the patrol and the scream of "Murder!" Here are to be found three great miserable slum districts, the glare of the low theatre, stifling and wretched dancehalls and suicides."

Yet it was not the city's sin that bothered Sam, but his own inner temptation to evil—pride. A life that had been and could be and might be rose to taunt him. In Boston he had many friends from his old student and preaching days—friends who had known not only his ability but his pride in it. It would be Calvary! And it was—but not in the way he had envisioned.

A remembrance of days past in Boston helped him, too. So many blessings, so many assurances of the power of this Army of salvation. One came from one of his earliest contacts. He wrote of the experience in *The Conqueror:* "A few years ago, in Boston, I attended an *'All Night of prayer,'* led by General Booth.[7] It was a blessed time, and scores of people sought the blessing of a clean heart. The Scriptures were read, many prayers were offered, many excellent things said, but there is only one I now remember, burning itself into my memory. Just before the meeting closed, Colonel Dowdle,[8] speaking to those who went to the penitent-form,[9] said, 'Remember, if you want to retain a clean heart, don't argue!' There were 20 years of practical holiness back of that advice, and it fell on my ears like the voice of God."

On October 12, 1888, son George was born to Sam and Lily—so frail that Lily's physician feared the Boston winter for him, especially in the drafty Brengle quarters, and it was decided that he would go to Amenia for the winter, to be cared for by Aunt Sarah. A few months later, he caught measles and for years his life was in jeopardy.

The Salvation Army building was on a narrow, noisy street in the poorest quarter of Boston's west end, Russell and Cambridge Streets, across the street from one of the most disreputable saloons in the city. Both quarters and hall were upstairs and were very dark. Yet the place grew to be heaven for Sam and Lily. They were supremely happy together, drew immense crowds to their meetings

---

7. General Booth's Boston visit during 1885, at which time Brengle was a Boston University theological student.

8. Commissioner James Dowdle, A.D.C. to General Booth.

9. Salvation Army term for altar.

and initiated a series of meetings that allowed them to know the joy of companionship and worship with persons who, like themselves, believed in a life that could be wholly victorious. Sam started what he called "United Holiness Meetings" which soon began to attract people from many denominations and a wide geographic area. Boston #1 became a mecca of many of the most prominent holiness teachers and preachers of New England. "As I look back," wrote Colonel Malcom Salmond, Army reporter who attended some of the services, "I can see many of those illustrious men and women, their garments soiled from kneeling on the plain hard floor stained by the tread of a thousand sinners' feet. The poor and illiterate, too, helped to crowd those meetings. Hundreds of those who attended have since dated their 'higher' religious experience from those days."

On the open street that holiness was tested. The Army was not allowed to march the street with any music whatsoever. Salvationists in authority in the Boston area had appeared before the police commissioners with a petition for the removal of such restriction, only to be met with silent contempt. The Brengles felt they must reach the "whosoever" in some strong manner so they devised silent marches, broken not by music but by quotations of Scripture commands, invitations, warnings, and promises, together with exhortations and testimonies. "These," said Sam, "were a very fair substitute for music, but my wife was not satisfied with only marching, so she organized a sandwich brigade[10] of about a dozen soldiers. This added to the attraction of our musicless marches, and brought people to our hall."

Thus for some time they continued from victory to victory. Then one night Sam suffered a particularly vicious interruption from a drunken visitor from across the street. He tried to reason

---

10. Assumed to be "sandwich boards" tied front and back to uniformed Salvationists, and printed with provocative Biblical statements.

with and quiet the man who only became more vocal, disruptive, and violent. Sam asked him to leave. He wouldn't. Sam then left the platform and, taking the man by the arm, gently escorted him to the door. Then he returned to the pulpit and finished his meeting. At the conclusion, hurrying downstairs, Sam appeared in the doorway on the ground level, whereupon the incensed man, waiting within ten feet of the door, hurled a whole paving brick. The brick struck Sam's head with full force, smashing it against the doorpost.

The Boston ministry was ended, and for a long time it seemed as if Sam's stay on earth was about to be ended also. For weeks he hovered between life and death. But he lived, though incapacitated for 18 months. He was sent away for special medical treatment, then, under strictest orders, sent back to Amenia with Lily to see if he could recover sufficiently for Salvation Army service. There were no pension, sick benefit, or retirement provisions in pioneer days.

This was a period of blinding temptation for both Sam and Lily. Sam, determined to be useful, began to write articles on spiritual living for the *War Cry* and other Salvation Army publications, his faith and intense sense of purpose prevailing. Lily, with the burden of a sick husband and two ailing children, plus care of her father, was not so fortunate. There was baby George, as frail and delicate as a baby could be, and tiny Elizabeth, born November 3, 1891, attacked by polio when eight months old and soon to develop tuberculosis.[11] She needed surgery but could not leave the family

---

11. Daughter Elizabeth, nicknamed "Duckie," remembers how her father counseled her to be a good soldier and count her blessings when she bemoaned her crippled body; how her mother insisted on the best medical treatment, on her becoming part of the life about her, not as a handicapped child but a well one, physical appearance to the contrary. Laboriously, Lily taught her how to use her facial muscles, which presented the most resistant problem, far more distressing than her affected arm and leg. The smile, in Elizabeth's words, remained "slightly crooked," and she cringed whenever a playmate would suddenly stare and say,

long enough to have it. Whatever would become of them all? How could she manage? Everyone seemed to be demanding her attention simultaneously. Where was her faith? Her ready smile, her infectious laugh? *Oh, dear God, where is Lily? The old believing, blithe Lily?* Some strange animate cloud of the spirit seemed to be blowing about—even in—her. Nothing, no one shone any more for Lily. She was always tired, always half ill, always running to answer a call that she had no strength or heart for. Lily! Lily? *Lily . . . Lily,* she questioned herself, *where are you going and why?*

She knew she must see a doctor but when her condition was diagnosed, she felt even worse. Due to a great number of shocks and too much burden and physical responsibility she was, the doctor stated, suffering from "melancholia," or at least was threatened with it. How dreadful! What business had a Christian with such a thing? But there it was, a force far stronger than herself that swept over her like a wave, quenching the light in her soul, and driving "every ray of sunshine out of her life."

What on earth to do, Lord? She kept going but the habitual burden only grew heavier. One day the old round of difficulties was going over and over in her mind: Sam's health; George's delicacy; her struggle to keep the baby alive. So tired. So very tired. She flung herself on her knees and cried out, *O Lord, You must help me. I can't go on like this. It's not Your will that I should, but I can't see any way out. Show me!*

One word flashed into her mind, as had two another day long ago:

REJOICE!

Rejoice? Lily was stunned. Rejoice? What for?

"What's wrong with your face? You smile funny!" Nevertheless, she had been taught to rejoice and rejoice she did, even if at times tears preceded faith. At 86 she is still rejoicing, and in a most sparkling humorous manner.

The word seemed to come closer, closer: REJOICE, REJOICE, REJOICE! Lily became absolutely still. What was the meaning of this? Stay still. Think. Listen. *Quieter, Lily. Quieter.* Shame began to creep over her.

"*O Lord,*" Lily prayed, "*I don't know what to rejoice about. Show me.*"

Then, like a bannered and bugled procession, a triumphant parade, her mercies passed before her. Husband alive; they could afford doctors; they had food and clothing, and their love for each other grew stronger and sweeter each day. As she counted up her blessings, she saw that nothing was lacking, that God had heaped up gifts and benefits, and she poured out praises and thanks till all gloom fled and a feeling of Christmas, or of Christmas Eve enveloped her and all about her.

"*Thank You! Thank You, Lord!*" shouted Lily inwardly and the last small scrap of darkness went tumbling into the night, never to come calling again. Sometimes the temptation to despond strode toward her down some dark alley of the spirit, for she was a delicate, nervous woman. Lack of sleep, overwork, anxiety about loved ones deeply affected her. But never again did she open either front or cellar door to the dark presence. And she never forgot how to drive away such a dangerous shadow:

REJOICE!   REJOICE!   REJOICE!

After Sam's recovery and for the next several years, until 1892, the Brengles served as District Officers for Maine and New Hampshire. Two and one-half years later on May 22, 1895, he took command as Divisional Officer for Western Massachusetts and Rhode Island, with headquarters in Worchester. Then, in 1896, the Brengles, like all other Salvationists in the United States, were dismayed and shocked with the announcement that made headlines across the country:

BALLINGTON BOOTHS HAVE WITHDRAWN!
MAY DIVIDE U.S. SALVATION ARMY!

Schism had again occurred. The young Booths had grown very much American and when ordered to proceed to another appointment, had resisted. They were then relieved of their command and seceded to organize the Volunteers of America, taking a great number of the faithful with them.

Sam wrote to officers in the United States: "A great calamity has fallen upon you, and a great sorrow upon the Army everywhere. . . . Your late beloved and honored commanders have refused to obey the General's orders and have resigned. . . . In this day of stern trial I call upon you to stand fast to God, to the world-wide purpose of The Army and to the flag. Be ready to suffer for the principles you have espoused."

Sam wrote his pledge of allegiance to Bramwell Booth, Chief of Staff: "If we humble our hearts and seek His face and look only to Him for deliverance, we shall live and yet 'delight ourselves in fatness.' It seems to me that now is the time to strike root, to deal with our own people, to lead them back to the old paths, to make them mighty in God."

He also wrote a number of articles for the *War Cry.* Together with earlier articles, written when he was recovering from the brick injury, they were printed in book form, entitled, *The Soul Winner's Secret.* Commenting on the value of the first Brengle book, Colonel George French, later to become a Commissioner, wrote: "This book probably did more to turn the minds of our people from self to souls, from the split to the Christ—thus saving them for The Salvation Army—than did any other person or agency."

Sam, true to type, put it this way: "Without the little brick there'd have been no little book." At home one day Lily painted this inscription on the offending brick: "As for you, ye meant it for evil, but God meant it for good to keep much people alive." Strange folk, the Brengles.

Sam and Lily had already known many separations but they could never have envisioned the next move. Told to leave "Mrs.

Brengle in charge of the district," Sam was now ordered because of the crisis to serve in Chicago, where the disruption had been catastrophic. The officer leader of the Midwestern forces had gone with the dissenters, abandoning hundreds of officers and soldiers to bewilderment and defeat. The new territorial leader, going to the Chicago headquarters, inquired of the doorman for the "person in charge," and was told, "I am." Sam was appointed second in command (General Secretary), for the North-Western Province which then comprised Illinois, Michigan, Wisconsin, and Indiana, and in the frequent necessary absences of the Provincial Commander held the forces together—interviewed, inspected, prayed with, commanded. He was then ordered to return east in June of 1896, to serve as General Secretary for the Central Chief Division with headquarters in New York City.

Here he served for 11 months without Lily, who now had to return to Amenia to tend her ailing father. The schism had long-reaching effects. The ranks were seriously depleted; many corps were lost entirely. Soldiers and officers were crushed and finances were "very hard." If ever The Salvation Army in America needed re-energizing it was now. Sam had only one answer—the experience of the "higher up" religion. This key, he felt, would unlock any door. By this time known throughout the country for his preaching and writing, Sam was ordered to the west coast to help revitalize the soldiery in a spiritual campaign.

Major William A. McIntyre, General Secretary for the Pacific Coast Chief Division, met him at the train and accompanied him to headquarters where they chatted. McIntyre seemed jittery, nervous. Finally he blurted, "Major, when I asked that you might come to California, I had a double purpose in mind. I wanted you for the Trestle Glen camp meetings, but I wanted you for myself as well. I've read your writings, sensed your spirit, and I believe you can help me. I've grown a little dry in my soul. I didn't expect to approach you here in the office. I intended rather to wait and lead the way to the penitent form at the camp. But I can't wait."

The two men got on their knees.

The Trestle Glen camp meetings blazed for two weeks with more than 400 people deciding to "live all out" for God. The next four weeks were given to short campaigns, and at the end of that period, McIntyre confided to Sam: "Brengle, since the camp meeting, Majors Marshall, Dunham,[12] and I have bound ourselves in a prayer covenant to pray that God would put you altogether in spiritual work. I'm writing Higgins[13] (the National Chief Secretary) to suggest strongly that you be used for this work exclusively."

Thus it was that Sam became what The Salvation Army terms "National Spiritual Special," an officer removed completely from organizational and administrative duties to deliver God's message. The night of his new appointment he wrote in his diary:

And Samuel grew and the Lord was with him and did let none of his words fall to the ground. And all Israel from Dan even to Beersheba knew that Samuel was established to be a prophet of the Lord (I Samuel 3:19-20).

Below the quotation he wrote: "What earthly honor or fame can compare with this! What dignity to be a 'prophet of the Lord!'"

Now he could see with what precision God had been preparing him for and leading him toward his destiny. But what about his darling Lily? What about little George and Elizabeth? He would be traveling continually. *Never home.* Sam could not think forward. He knew backward. He knew now. He could trust for forward. But his own darling little Lily. . . .

As for Lily, she had no decision to make, no cause to plead. The Salvation Army represented God's will to her, and God came first. That she knew loneliness, heaviness of spirit, some foreboding,

---

12. Col. Stephen Marshall, Lt. Col. David Dunham.
13. General Edward J. Higgins.

cannot be denied, but she knew that she was a conqueror through Christ, and she knew how to manage. She wrote to Sam of her experience in this manner:

When the time draws near for you to leave me, my heart begins to get heavy and restless. And then I go to God, and look up into His face, and ask Him to comfort me, and to take away my fears and heaviness, and accept my sacrifices for Him, and to bless you, and make you a blessing. And, Sam, He comes, and so floods my heart with His joy and peace that people think I don't care.

She did care, but she knew she had willingly become a Salvation Army soldier and she never flinched from the fight. Sam said later: "She rejoiced that she had something to sacrifice for her Saviour. She never grumbled or complained, or worried or perplexed me. But she rejoiced and believed and prayed, and was my most efficient helper, though the diameter of the globe lay between us. She was, indeed, my little heart's ease."

Lily reared Sam's children, one frail, one crippled. She cared for her aged father. She succored the needy by act and correspondence. And she upheld Sam in his far-flung ministry. Noting one of their many separations she wrote to a friend in later years: "Yes, Sam is going to Australia. He will leave on the 24th. Oh, you know how old letters will be when I get them, and that the grass might be green on his grave by the time one reaches me. I am not so brave as some women and I admit that the only one thing that could make me endure the separation is the certainty that he will make hundreds of homes happy and thousands of evil people good by his going. I have seen too much of the misery of the poor to stand in the way of his going, even though I feel that India and Africa may lie beyond Australia for him. . . ."

Another time, writing to Sam, she said of her eagerness but helplessness to aid him: ". . . but all of a sudden I remembered Jesus, and put you out of my hands into His in a flash, and then I was at rest. It was so beautiful to find that safe place in which to hide you. No one can reach you there. My own love is safe—safe."

She often quoted poetry to him in order to strengthen them both, noble statements such as this one by Sidney Lanier:

As the marsh hen secretly builds on the watery sod,
Behold, I will build me a nest on the greatness of God;
I will fly in the greatness of God as the marsh hen flies,
In the freedom that fills all the space twixt the marsh and the skies;
By so many roots as the marsh grass sends in the sod,
I will heartily lay me ahold of the greatness of God.

Sometimes, the poems were her own:

Dread miles of land and sea between us rise,
And hide thee from my reft and hungering eyes,
Yet when I turn to God in ardent prayer,
Lo! I behold thee! Thou abidest there.

Such perceptive expressions as this were continual: "I had to think twice to realize that you are not here. But you are just the other side of God, and *He is right here.* Hallelujah! Goodbye, my own Sam. I love and love you, and don't forget to pray for you. Your own loving Lily." Again, "I have followed you off in the carriage in my mind and traced you to Amenia. I have loafed about the station with you. I settled you on that train. But now I'm going to leave you somewhere near Pawling. It doesn't pay—it savors too much of parting. And we are *not* parting. You are in the presence of the Lord toward the sunrise, and I toward the sunset, but the same sun shines on us both."

Almost 20 years of sacrificial life, soldier life begun in 1896, with Sam and Lily almost always separated, yet they grew closer together, more and more attuned to each other until often their thoughts seemed united at great distances, their souls part of a single whole. Each knew physical distress and illness, life-long ailments, Sam's from that brick blow, Lily's from that chill when a teen-ager. But they never became burdenbearers. Early they had decided upon joy, and they never removed their allegiance from it.

Both were simple in their wisdom, childlike in their simplicity. A remark a neighbor made epitomizes both Sam's and Lily's lifetime attitude. Describing the way Lily attacked the most unpleasant life circumstances regarding her children, the neighbor commented, "It's always, 'Let's have a picnic.' I do like the way you make a spree out of the most disagreeable things. You have such a good time over them." Daughter Elizabeth says it was always thus. Sam and Lily were "picnic people."

That Lily, who possessed remarkable speaking and writing ability, lived a closeted life in later years is true. Yet there appears to have been no resentment, only gratitude for the opportunities she had, one of which was the rearing of George and Elizabeth. She believed strongly in mothers rearing their own children, and wrote to daughter Elizabeth after she was grown:

I do not know that I thank God oftener for any of His dealings with me after saving my soul and giving me my husband and children, than for his great mercy in shutting me up at home to care for those children. Only this month I have been reading all through the Bible how God brings children into being not by accident but by design, and how He takes pains to prepare their mothers; and it is so clear that when He has done this He means the mother to take care of them and not leave them to others . . . but how many of us when our Father puts children into our hands, coolly turn them over to another woman, and set ourselves about some other work. I feel no criticism for anyone who feels or acts differently, nor ever have. I saw and acted differently myself once. But since God has shut me in I have studied principles in His Book and find great peace and joy in living them out. A child's morals and manners as well as its spirituality are determined by the atmosphere of the home, not by an occasional half hour spent with it or by any number of lectures or preachments. A woman once asked me if I were not at home a great deal with my children. I said yes. "I thought so," she said. "One can always tell by a child's face and ways when it is trained by its own mother."

Daughter Elizabeth knew great physical pain during her child-hood and teen years, a fact which distressed her parents immensely. Lily would write to Sam: "We have gone quietly on today. Eliza-beth's back hurt her pretty badly." After being told by Lily that Elizabeth, due to her pain and deformity felt that God did not love her, Sam wrote while in Upsala, Sweden, in March of 1906:

My darling Elizabeth, my precious girl:

Mother wrote me that you are sometimes tempted to believe that God does not love you, else He would not have allowed you to be so afflicted. This, my darling, is an old temptation, as old as Job. His wife told him to curse God and die, but Job replied, "Thou speakest as one of the foolish women speaketh. What? Shall we receive good at the hand of God, and shall we not receive evil? In all this did not Job sin with his lips." And later he said, "Though He slay me yet will I trust Him."

The truth is, darling, that your afflictions may prove to be your greatest blessings, and they *will be*, if you will believe God when He says: "All things work together for good to them that love God," and "Our light affliction, which is but for a moment [as compared with eternity] worketh for us a far more exceeding and eternal weight of glory." I have learned to praise God for my afflictions, for "whom the Lord loveth He chasteneth." I don't always understand how God makes trouble and affliction work for good, but I believe what He says and not my feelings.

Jeremiah said, "It is good for a man to bear the yoke in his youth" (Lamentations 3:27). I have found it so, and so will you. It is like taming a colt. It saves it much pain when it gets full grown to have been broken young. Our afflictions are our yoke. They are God's way of training us. Believe, be obedient, trust Him and you will yet praise Him for all the way He leads you. God bless you, my sweet girl!

As the children grew, the family bonds of love seemed to tighten, rather than loosen, though now the members resided in four places: Sam on the road, George in college, first as an under-graduate at Wesleyan University in Middletown, Connecticut; then at Harvard Law School in Boston; Elizabeth at Centenary Col-legiate Institute; and Lily at the old homestead.

Besides having a probing legal mind, George wrote poetry. About his regard for his sister he observed:

AFTERGLOW

When the splendor of sunset has faded
From the rim of the western hill;
When the roseate hues have all vanished,
And the world grows peaceful and still,
Then the afterglow creeps o'er the landscape
E'er the final coming of night,
And the sky is all tinted with glory
From the unseen fountain of light.

Like the deep afterglow is her beauty,
Not sparkling, but peacefully fair.
And it lights up her face with its brightness,
And her halo of gold-brown hair.
For her heart is a heart of pure sunshine,
Where never a cloud is known,
And the calm brightness which lightens her face
In that heart has its unseen home.

Another poem, written to Lily and titled, "O Little Mother of
Mine," was set to music and popularized by famed tenor, John
McCormick:

Sometimes in the hush of the evening hour,
When the shadows creep from the west,
I think of the twilight songs you sang
And the boy you lulled to rest;
The wee little boy with the tousled head,
That so long ago was thine,
I wonder if sometimes you long for that boy,
O little mother of mine.

And now he has come to man's estate,
Grown stalwart in body and strong,
And you'd hardly know that he was the lad
Whom you lulled with your slumber song.
The years have altered the form and the life,
But his heart is unchanged by time,
And still he is only the boy as of old,
O little mother of mine.

Sam had longed and prayed that George would become a Salvation Army officer and was disappointed when he decided on law, but the affinity was so strong between the two that when the decision was made, it too became a source of joy to Sam. Many years later George recounted: "My father was extremely anxious that I, his son, should preach the Gospel. When I finally decided on the law as a profession, I told him that the Bible said: 'Watch and pray,' and I suggested that we whack the job up between us. He said he would be content to see me devote my life to the law provided I would always be a good lawyer. And by *good* he did not mean successful. *Good* to him meant the all-pervading righteousness that exalteth an individual as well as a nation."

As is often the case with Salvationist parents, Sam was unable to attend George's graduation from law school, being on campaign in Tasmania. He wrote:

My darling George:

If I were a man of the world, I should be mighty proud of you and of your recent record in college, but since I am not a worldling, I am profoundly grateful that you have come out with such flying colors. But "honor bright," do you think you deserved Phi Beta Kappa? Didn't you captivate and hypnotize those kindly old profs with your winsome smile?

I was glad to learn that Gilbert Swift and Edgar came to see you graduate and hear you speak. I can imagine how Edgar's eyes gleamed and danced and how he had to hug himself to keep himself reasonably quiet when you won the prize. . . . Mother seems to feel that you so far surpassed the other fellows that she considered Brown was right when he said to her that you were first, so far first that there wasn't any second. . . . I am praying for you daily, darling George, that you may know God, love Him, and delight yourself in Him. I don't think I am praying any longer that you may be any Army officer, or preacher, but that you may know God and delight to do His will. God's will runs through all honorable, legitimate human employments—the highest employment of man is that of the prophet, so it seems to me—God's mouthpiece. But this I know, my precious George, He does not want to lose you. He wants your friendship and to be your companion, your counselor, your Guide, your Comforter, your Teacher, your helper, your Savior and the inheritance of your soul forever—your *other and divine self*. Don't disappoint Him, don't send Him sorrowfully away. Don't keep Him standing and knocking, while you are engaged with a hundred trifling things that will in the end leave your poor soul hungry and thirsty and atrophied. Throw the door of your will and affection open and cry out, "Come in, my Lord! Come in!"

Mother has written me that you had a big fit of the blues after she and Elizabeth left Middletown. Don't I understand that! I certainly do. Didn't Moses Slaughter stand on the tail end of the train and weep and didn't I stand down below and look up at him feeling just about too bad to weep, when we said goodbye, after graduation. He went off home to his two sisters and I went—well, really I don't remember where I did go. I didn't go home for I had no home and no home folks. I guess I went off to my rented room. My father wasn't on the other side of the world. He had gone to the other worlds, and mother too, and I was alone and lonely and blue.

I was poor. I didn't have anything and indeed, I was somewhat in debt. But I was young and the world was before me and God was for me. So I cheered myself up as best I could, sought the Lord, followed His leadings and He blessed me and has so for 27 years, making me glad and prospering me in my work.

The blues can arise from various causes . . . but after all, the soul is so wonderful, so nearly divine, and is so shut up and imprisoned within its little house of flesh and bones that no mere human fellowship can meet its needs and its unsatiable hunger. No one, not even a mother, a wife, the dearest friend, can come into the soul's small house and live with it. It lives alone. It has its hopes, its fears, its unutterable longings and aspirations, its solemn hours in darkness and stillness, which no human being can wholly share or understand. This but proves that the soul needs a divine fellow, and the worst kind of blues and indeed the aggravation of any fit of the blues arises from the failure of complete and glad correspondence between the soul and this divine other self, who is God in Christ.

He came to me in Boston, when I was lonely and half sick and depressed and in debt and I couldn't see hardly a step ahead and He flooded me with light and love and peace and a sense of tenderest, sweetest, most intelligent fellowship, and I cried out in joy. It is a real experience, darling boy. Madame Guyon had it. Read her hymn written in the dark and awful Bastille, when not a friend was allowed to see her. Paul had it. Mother has it, and *you* may have it.

I have no genius for religion. I was a pagan. I envied people who I thought had a natural bent for goodness and religion. I was dark and corrupt, but He came and flooded me with light. God bless and bless you, my precious boy!

Read John 14 on your knees, slowly and prayerfully, and notice especially verses 14 to 27.[14]

In November, 1908, Lily's father, an astute exemplar of Christ, greatly loved by the family and treasured during the many years Lily had tended him died. Writing soon after to Elizabeth, Lily said:

Grandpa would have been 91 years old today. The Lord mercifully took him home. I'm glad that he is well and strong and happy beyond our power to imagine, and that his days of mourning are ended. He lives, darling! He came to see us on the north piazza that night, and he found us safe, and well, and happy in Jesus. And if he is sent often to revisit us, he will always find us happy in the Lord. I hope he will find my darling girl so too.

Of this experience Elizabeth recalls:

Some might call this an hallucinatory experience. It was not so. Nor was it an exaggerative one. Mama was not given either to ghost watching, lack of discernment, imaginative exaggeration or any other impractical pursuit. She was always searching for the truth and did not seek emotional self-satisfaction. What happened, I believe, is true. What tag is given it is insignificant. There are times when God breaks through to us in extra-sensory ways. If we choose we may accept them. If we desire to disparage, we reject and are the poorer for it.

Anyhow, shortly after Grandpa's death, a girl friend and I were sleeping on the north porch, the piazza, and were unawakened when mother came to check on us and was met by Grandpa. As she described his advent he was a vital presence. He wanted to tell her that the rules of Heaven were about the same as here, that he knew great contentment and happiness and that he wanted people here to know the eternal verities are sure.

---

14. When George retired from law, he was senior partner of Bigham, Englar, Jones, and Houston, 44 Wall Street, New York. He married Maude Catherine Jackson, daughter of Salvation Army officers.

Lily wrote of the parting:

> I cannot touch your lips, your hand,
> Again while time shall last.
> But when I look within my heart,
> I hold you fast! I hold you fast!

And in a subsequent letter to Elizabeth:

Darling, while I was making a bed upstairs a bit ago, a line from one of Tennyson's songs in "The Princess" came to mind. I don't know why. Perhaps from a glimpse of Mama's pictured face on my dressing bureau: "Oh, death in life, the days that are no more!"

It gives one heart pangs to believe such stuff as that. The bygone days were beautiful and they are gone forever. But that's nothing to mourn for. With God there are far, far better days before us. I thank Him for the old house, the old days and my father and mother. But His law of nature is: "Instead of your fathers shall be your children."

Her mind seemed often to focus on eternity now, on dying, heaven, all matters eternal. She wrote Sam (regarding their rank of Brigadier):

I've got fond of that hideous title because it was yours. I like whatever you are, and love you no matter what people call you . . . some day I'll have you always in sight! I read what Jesus said about not marrying in heaven without any fears the other day. It won't be like this earth, but I shall have you there in some way which satisfies, God has made all our happiness here, and He won't be less mindful of us there.

When the children were in their late teens, and away at school, Lily sometimes was able to accompany Sam on his campaigns in the States. She rejoiced in the journeys, but sorrowed when she was not with the children on special occasions. On Elizabeth's twentieth birthday she wrote:

My precious darling girl:
    Father hurried off a birthday letter to you this morning to catch you by the third, and gave me no time to write too. Someone says you're the

image of me and I am flattered again. I'm a proud mother. Some girls are silly enough to mind being 20. I don't know why. Most women are better looking at 40 than at 20, and certainly they are wiser and happier. I suppose girls feel, when they are 20, that they can't be children any longer. But they can! I'm a child still, at heart, and Grandpa was, to the last. You have gained one of the heights of life, and can look down as well as up, but there is no danger, no necessary regret and life at "sweet and twenty" should be still and is—the springtime.

God means every decade to be the best, until the last. I pray that you may carry out His purpose for your soul, and Father and I love you better as you grow older. I suppose God doesn't, because He loved you with His might from the beginning, but He can make you realize His love more and more as you grow older. Let Him do that, my treasure girl.[15]

Regarding childlikeness, Sam and Lily again agreed. In an article on "Emotionality," Sam wrote:

Sanctification is not purely an emotional experience. It is equally volitional. But you cannot, however, have any great inner experience without emotion. A young man cannot fall in love with a sweet girl without deep emotion stirring within him. . . . People forget themselves. They cease to be standardized and every man expresses himself according to his temperament and the emotion that is surging within him.

One of the great dangers to religion today is the fear, probably born of pride that people have of emotion. They are so anxious to be balanced and well poised that they cease to be vital and natural. The highest religious experiences make men and women as natural as little children and each one will express himself according to his own temperament. Some are naturally quiet, others are demonstrative. . . .

In the Brengle family, childlikeness remained a fact, a goal ("Except ye become as a little child ye shall not see the Kingdom of Heaven") and the binding adventure of four adults. The immediate was cherished as a child cherishes; but also, and increasingly for

---

15. Elizabeth married Chester Reed, a neighbor since childhood. Together, they spent a lifetime farming near Pawling and Amenia, New York. They have one son, Logan, married to Marilyn Mack. The Logan Reeds have four children.

Lily, the treasure to come was relished. She wrote to Sam on January 31, 1914:

I often think about Heaven. I have in the past but in a vague fashion. I have rather formed the viewpoint concerning what I had to leave, to get there. But today, it seemed to be such a wonderful home going! My home with you couldn't seem any more definite, personal, and delightful than my home with God. I hope that vision may abide with me, for it seems the true one.

In her small, rather obscure handwriting, Lily sent a birthday tribute to Sam, marked "author unknown, sentiment applied to Samuel Logan Brengle, and endorsed and multiplied by all the other Brengles of his quartette." It describes the affection and family unity of the "quartette":

> This is your birthday. On the calendar
> Of those who know you it is marked with gold,
> As both a holy and a holiday.
> You make us happy, and you make us good,
> By simply being with you. You bestow,
> And think you are receiving; like a rose
> That marvels at the fragrance of the breeze.
> We are most glad, since you were sent to earth,
> It was while we are here; not hastened down
> To shine amid the shadows of the past.
> Nor kept to grace some joyful future day;
> But come to share our present as it is,
> And leave tomorrow better for your stay.

During 1915, after an especially vigorous campaign, the first "home" appointment since 1896 came to Sam: he was appointed to command the school for officers training in New York. The Brengles were ecstatic. *Home!* The children were now grown, and it was a work in which Lily could help. Home!

Sam had been ailing for some time. Stomach? Intestines? Colon? Appendicitis? No one was quite sure, and though an operation for appendicitis appeared at first to reach his trouble, it failed. Lily wrote Eileen Douglas, who had lived in the home for years: "I came home from that hospital the happiest woman on earth and just treading on air." But the apparent recovery lasted only a short time and Sam had to reenter the hospital. Diagnosis: bleeding stomach ulcers.

Elizabeth was with Lily. She went to bed her usual courageous self but was found in the morning sobbing over her inability to button her dress. They were appalled. Tears from their little mother? The condition first was diagnosed as acute nervous prostration and though medicine seemed somewhat to restore her, she was ordered to bed and grew worse. Tumor on the brain? Hardening of the arteries? No one was sure. Whatever it was, suffering was acute. Soon, Lily slipped into semi-consciousness. The doctors told Sam he probably would not see her alive again. She was moved to a little sanitarium for women in Castile, New York, a village about 65 miles southwest of Rochester. Sam, though very ill, had a room across the street but was forced to return to New York for another very serious operation. George had just graduated and came out on weekends.

"The devil came against me," Sam wrote, "with a great army of troubles and fears, and perplexities and threatening disasters, and in the lonely hours of the still nights he fought with me. Day by day I had the victory; night after night he returned to assault. But he was defeated. Utterly routed!"

For a time, Lily slipped in and out of consciousness, rallied and conversed. Once she said to Elizabeth, who had burst into tears at thought of her mother leaving her: "My darling, come here to my arms! (She could hardly raise them.) You can never lose me!" She sent this poem to her sister-in-law, Bessie Yount:

A SOUL MELODY OF LIFE'S TWILIGHT

> Some say that I am dying,
> They know not what they say;
> For never was I living,
> One whit more than today.

And some day they will tell you
That I am lying dead;
But think it not, for only
My spirit shall have fled.

'Tis all so very simple,
Or so it seems to me,
This body's just my dwelling,
A little while to be.

When my house is empty,
And closed its windows are,
You must not think you've lost me,
For I shall not be far.

Just think of me as living,
And this small earthly home
As changed for one in Heaven
Beside my Saviour's throne.

                                                    —Anon

Sam did see Lily again, being allowed a visit from the hospital. Death seemed on tiptoe but imperative. She lingered for almost four months. Sam watched and loved and wrote, "The nurse wondered at her patience and gentle resignation during those months of wasting. She ceased to speak during those last weeks and seldom gave any sign of recognition."

Elizabeth remembers:

The Sunday before she died, God let her come to full consciousness without pain. The four of us visited, talked of old times. She and Father had family prayers, as they always did when the four of us were home, and it was a beautiful day to remember, except that it was almost too poignant to bear. That night sleep took her into the coma which lasted till within five minutes of the end. Catholics have a theory that hearing stays with a dying person after all other senses have dimmed. Father kissed her, quoted Scripture, prayed and talked to her as he did in the old happy days when they were sweethearts, and no one else in all the world were near. There was not the faintest flicker of response.

Less than five minutes before the final quick little breath was drawn and loosed, Sam leaned over her and said, almost in desperation, "Darling, is Jesus with you?"

Elizabeth recalls: "Quickly, clearly, and strongly, came back the definite reply, 'Yes!' And she was gone. It was like a voice from the other world, from Heaven, like someone on the far bank of a river, calling back to us and telling us that all was well."

Sam wrote her sister Susie:

Then she fell asleep in Jesus as peacefully and unafraid as ever her tired babies fell asleep in her mother arms, out of our presence into the open vision of her Lord, where I could not for the present follow, but the blessings of which I seemed and still seem in some indefinable and divinely consoling sense to share.

Every other foundation seemed swept away in the rising flood, but Jesus stood sure. A few months before she had written a prophetic testimony in words to the tune of "My Rosary":

> And when my days on earth are done,
> Heaven's morning breaks and shadows flee,
> When just before me waits the judgment throne,
> Earth's last dread hour I'll spend, dear Lord, with Thee.

Elizabeth remembers:

I had always been a strong believer in immortality, but this was divine proof. For months past, watching her sink, I had the desperate feeling that our little family circle was being broken. She was so weak and helpless, her spirit burdened with pain and sickness, cramped so to speak, like a body swathed in bandages. Now, suddenly, I had the feeling that she was free and thus had emerged into God's sunlight, and like Lazarus had cast off the shroud and come forth at the bidding of the Lord. In some strange, mystic way, she seemed near at hand, though unseen, and the little family circle whole again. I missed the visual contact with her beyond words—but still I have always felt that she is very much alive in another of God's houses, and not too far away at that.

Of those final moments, Sam recounted:

I feared for Elizabeth. She knelt on one side and I on the other (George
was on his way). You know, Susie, what a mother's child she has been and
she had been worn by months of sorrowful watching, but as those last
small sighs came she looked across at me, with a face radiant as the
morning and said, "She's happy, so happy. And oh, I've got her again now. I
seemed to have lost her all these weeks, but she is with us now as never
before," and it seemed as though the glory into which little Mother was
sweeping was reflected in the transformed face of my precious child."

At the funeral, presided over by Commander Evangeline Booth,
George spoke in tribute for Elizabeth and himself. In part he
confided:

I love to think of the Fifth Commandment, the commandment to "Honor
thy father and thy mother," as being just between the commandments
that deal with our relations to God and those that deal with our relations
with our fellow men, because I think that the relationship between mother
and children partakes of the divine. I know that our relationship did. She
taught us about God, and there was no phase in our relationship of which
she did not make God a part. I used to think of her as being *one of the thoughts
of God*—as almost a little piece of God here on earth—and I shall so think of
her always. Somehow, I've never been able to think of God except through
Mother. I reached out to God through her and I thought of Him in terms of
her. It was because of her and through her that I came to love God, and
somehow she represented God here on earth to me, and she embodied and
made real my ideas of Him. I thought of God through mother and of
mother through God. I went out to the penitent-form in a General's
meetings and became a Christian largely because I knew it would make
her happy above all things on earth. It was the thought of her and the
longing to make her happy that led me to God, and the memory of her is
going to keep me close to Him.

. . . She has gone home to that house of many mansions that He went
to prepare and somehow it seems to be right next door. It isn't cold or
unreal or far away since Mother is gone—it's home.

She was only a little mother. I used to tuck her under my arm, and her head only came to my shoulder. And now that she has gone to Heaven I mourn for her more than I can tell. But I mourn not as one without hope, for I know, oh I know, I know, that somewhere in that house of many mansions in God's own good time, I shall tuck that little mother of mine under my arm and tell her that I love her! And till then I can say from my heart, as I know she would have me, that "Death is swallowed up in victory!"

After Sam had publicly spoken, "pulled in the net and got a number of people to the penitent-form," and sat down beside him, George whispered, "Father, I've got part of the glory. It's come!"

A few days before Lily died, because her hands had become greatly swollen, her wedding ring had to be removed. Sam said of that sad incident: "I was present when the jeweler cut off the symbol of our tender love and union. . . . It seemed as though he were cutting into my heart. But when I took the little ring and read the inscription I had engraved within it 28 years before, my heart rejoiced. It was *Holiness Unto The Lord.* That was Lily's secret—and mine."

Sam marched steadfastly forward, girdling the globe with his message of inner peace, of God's love, for another 20 years, never really at home anywhere from that time forward—hotel rooms; officers' quarters, a special counseling room; the pulpit. Sometimes the Army assigned a young officer to travel with him as soloist and secretary. Remarkable friendships were forged. So it was that in spring, 1919, when World War I had ended and America was bent on speed and sound and serendipidy, that Sam received a phone call during one of his rest periods in son George's home:

"Colonel, we think we've found an apt young man for you. Will you be kind enough to interview Captain Earl Lord? He's young, quick, writes a good letter and has a remarkably resonant baritone voice."

"Of course," said Sam. "Send him along."

APPENDIX

Sam's Favorite Scripture

Almost the entire Bible seemed to be Sam's favorite, but here are a few verses that he often quoted:

> Enter the temple gates with thanksgiving;
> Go into its courts with praise.
> Give thanks to Him and praise Him.
> The Lord is good;
> His love is eternal and
> His faithfulness lasts forever.
> —Psalm 100:4–5

Deeply moved, once more, Jesus went to the tomb, which was a cave with a stone placed at the entrance. "Take the stone away!" Jesus ordered.—John 11:38

Believe me when I say that I am in the Father, and the Father is in me. If not, believe because of the things I do. I am telling you the truth: whosoever believes in me will do what I do—yes, he will do even greater things, because I am going to the Father.—John 14:11

Let us, then hold firmly to the faith we profess. For we have a great High Priest who has gone into the very presence of God—Jesus, the Son of God.—Hebrews 4:14

I [Jesus] have told you this so that my joy may be in you and that your joy may be complete. My commandment is this: love one another, just as I love you.—John 15:11

Do not be afraid, little flock, for your Father is pleased to give you the Kingdom.—Luke 12:32

A Poem by Lily

The following poem is assumed to have been written by Lily:

> *Following*
>
> "Wilt thou, then, feed my lambs?
> Lovest thou Me?"
> Give me Thy neediest;
> Theirs would I be.

Exile and strangerhood,
These for their meed,
Mine be the country, Lord,
Where Thy steps lead.

Sad in their darkness,
Mourn thee thine own,
So mourned the angels, once
Thy vacant throne!

Father and Mother thine,
Lov'st thou no more?
Daughter of Heaven, O Lord,
Thee I adore.

Far have I put from thee,
Lover and friend,
By Thy lone cross, Lord,
Lonely I bend.

Those who have loved thee
Pray for thy death,
He whom Thou trustedst Lord,
Sold Thy last breath.

What if thy following
Won thee no Heaven?
Heaven *is* following,
To the death even!

Lily's Rice Pudding

Mrs. Brigadier Ernest Holz, now in her 90's, remembers the recipe for the oldfashioned rice pudding that was a stand-by in quarters cooking, and when the Brengles visited the Holz family, they brought along their recipe.

½ C rice	1 qt. milk
⅓ C sugar	½ t salt
1 t grated lemon peel	¼ t nutmeg
⅓ C seedless raisins	

Combine rice, milk, sugar, and salt; pour into buttered 1 ½ qt. baking dish. Bake in slow oven (300 deg.) 1 hour; stir occasionally. Add lemon peel, nutmeg and raisins; continue baking additional 1½ to 1¾ hours. ⅔ C brown sugar may be used in place of granulated sugar. Makes six servings.

Lily's Favorite Quotations

Following are quotations from *The Vision of His Face,* a book beloved by Lily during the last years. Written by Dora Farcomb, it was published by American Tract Society.

The Word of God is severe in its demands; but though it is a sharp sword, that cuts and lays bare the deepest motives hidden in the heart, it is with the merciless severity of merciful love.

The Good Physician really heals the leprosy of sin. He does not only salve the wound, but the flesh is restored as the flesh of a little child.

We dare not approach God with a lie on our lips, or ask Him to free us from a sin that we are not really fighting against, a sin that we secretly love. . . . And besides sorrow we must face restitution. If you have told a lie, then you must untell it; and if you have stolen something, you must give it back; if you have taken away someone's character, you must do something to restore it.

Let us get up every morning with this for the instantaneous thought, that my Master wakes me. I wake, I rise, His property.

The secret of perpetual peace: The possibility of going to Christ about everything is illustrated in the story of some weavers who were working in an eastern palace. They wondered to see a little child among them whose work always went smoothly on, without a break or a snarl in the thread. Theirs continually got frayed and broken. They asked, and the child answered, "I only go and tell the King." They declared that they reported to Him once a week. "But," she said softly, "I go and get the knot untied at the first little tangle."

It is good now and again for you to be without a taste for God,
That you be not puffed up in days when all is fair,
And take some pleasure in yourself that you are what you are not.

It is a truism that we grow slowly but surely into the likeness of the people we admire and deliberately associate with. No one can walk with God, eagerly and persistently without helping others to see His face more clearly.

My Own

I do not own an inch of land,
But all I see is mine—
The orchard and the mowing fields,
The lawns and gardens fine,
The winds my tax collectors are,
They bring me tithes divine—
Wild scents and subtle essences,
A tribute rare and free;
And, more magnificent than all,
My window keeps for me
A glimpse of blue immensity—
A litle strip of sea.

—Anon

The Street Preacher

No crowd encircled him about.
He stood despised with two or three,
But like a spring in summer drought,
The word he uttered, quickened me.

Around us Oxford, dome and tower,
Majestic, breathed her charm august;
But which of all her spells had power
To raise the wretched from the dust?

What Oxford could not, Jesus did,
Bared to my eyes the depths of grace,
And all the unguessed treasures hid
Beneath the dust of commonplace.

Since then I tread the pilgrim's way,
Still plodding on through sun and rain,
But, like a star shines out that day,
The day which saw me born again.

—C. Field

I Saw a Child

I saw a child
With drooping mouth and lids still wet,
Today,
Lie fast asleep, too grieved to play;

I knew of a fair gift in store for him,
Before which sorrow's memory would grow dim,
And watching him, I smiled.

My own eyes close;
Dull, unexpectant, wistful 'neath the rod,
I fall asleep. It may be God,
Forseeing some undreamed of joy for me,
Ev'n now smiles to Himself all tenderly
O'er the glad thing He knows.

—Anon

April Rain

It is not raining rain for me,
It's raining daffodils,
In ev'ry dimpled drop I see
Wild flowers on the hills.

The clouds of gray engulf the day,
And overwhelm the town,
It is not raining rain to me,
It's raining roses down.

It is not raining rain to me,
But fields of clover bloom,
Where any buccaneering bee
Can find a bed and room.

A health unto the happy,
A fig for him who frets,
It is not raining rain to me,
It's raining violets.

—Robert Loveman

The following quotations from Tennyson were underlined by Sam in 1915, probably after Lily left him for Gloryland.

For woman is not undeveloped man,
But reverse; could we make her as the man,
Sweet love were slain; his dearest bond is this,
Not like to like, but like in difference.
Yet in the long years like must they grow;
The man be more of woman, she of man;
He gain in sweetness and in moral height,

Nor lose the wrestling sinews that throw the world;
She mental breadth, nor fail in childward care,
Nor lose the childlike in the larger mind;
Till at the last she set herself to man,
Like perfect music unto noble words;
And so these twain, upon the skirts of time,
Sit side by side, full-summed in all their powers,
Dispensing harvest, sowing the to be,
Self reverent each and reverencing each,
Distinct in individualities,
But like each other even as those who love,
Then comes the statelier Eden back to men;
Then reign the world's great bridals, chaste and calm;
Then springs the crowning race of human kind,
May these things be!

I Must Work

And I must work thro' months of toil
And years of cultivation,
Upon my proper path of soil
To grow my own plantation;
I'll take the showers as they fall,
I will not vex my bosom;
Enough if at the end of all
A little garden blossom.

Where Thou Art Not

So find I every pleasant spot
In which we two were wont to meet,
The field, the chamber and the street,
For all is dark where thou art not.

This Life

The life that almost dies in me;
That dies not, but endures with pain
And lowly forms the firmer mind
Treasuring the look it cannot find,
The words that are not heard again.

Found among Lily's clippings.

In the Morning

"Cause me to hear Thy lovingkindness
in the morning"—Psalm 43:8

A dangerous time is the morning!
There is nothing to fear at night;
Calm are the eyes in closing,
Tired of the urgent light;
The body is healed in sleeping,
Trouble and labor cease,
The soul is in God's safe keeping,
The heart is in perfect peace.

But who can say in the morning
How fierce will the trials be?
What difficult paths may be trodden,
What griefs may encompass me?
The whole wide world is sunlighted;
But I see not an hour before
What new, strange sorrows or dangers
The future may have in store.

O speak to me in the morning,
Lord, of my every day!
Thou art my great Director
As I pass to the hidden way;
If I hear Thy voice in the morning,
I open the day with song,
Forth shall I go to conquer,
Thy presence shall make me strong.
                         —Marianne Farmingham

One of Lily's favorites.

My Beloved Ones

Lord, make me one with Thine own faithful ones,
Thy saints who love Thee and are loved by Thee;
Till the day break and till the shadows flee
At one with them in alms and orisons;
At one with him who toils and him who runs,
And him who yearns for union yet to be;

At one with all who throng the crystal sea,
And wait the setting of our moons and suns,
Ah, my beloved ones gone on before,
Who looked not back with hand upon the plough!
If beautiful to me while still in sight,
How beautiful must be your aspects now,
Your unknown, well-known aspects in that light
Which clouds shall never cloud forevermore.

                        —Christiana Rossetti

Beloved Motto

Jesus is the Head of this house;
The unseen Guest at every meal;
The silent Listener to every conversation.

If

And everywhere, here and always
If we would but open our eyes,
We should find through these beaten footpaths
Our way into Paradise.
Dull earth would be dull no longer,
The clod would sparkle a gem;
And our hands, at their commonest labor,
Would be building Jerusalem.

                        —Anon

Surprise

I never thought it could be thus,
Month after month to know
The river of Thy peace without
One ripple in its flow;
Without one quiver in the trust,
One flicker in its glow.

                        —Anon

The following is a condensation of an article appearing in the U.S. WAR
CRY, August 20, 1887, regarding George Washington, "ex-slave from
Danbury, Ct."

Our brother was born in the year 1841, in Andrews County, Va. His
parents were slaves, whose poor living and hard work with plenty of

whipping combined to keep down their spirits. Sometimes they would wish to be free, but it was only a wish, for there was no hope. When the war broke out, whispers went around that something wonderful was about to happen. If they were caught discussing freedom

THEY WERE FLOGGED.

George, with others, was sent by his slave-master to Richmond to make entrenchments but George, watching his opportunity,

RAN AWAY,

was caught and brought back, and got a good whipping. Shackles were put on his legs at night and on his waist in the day time. Then he was sent to Drury's Bluff, Va., where he made a successful try for freedom and served three years in the U.S. Navy. The first prayer he ever remembers was at the hospital in Williamsburg, so ill he did not expect to live. He prayed God to save his life and he would serve Him forever but

GEORGE FORGOT HIS PROMISE

and now kept a place in Reading, Ct., for the sale of cider and wine to Bethel and Danbury hatters. Occasionally thoughts would turn to his promise. One day while drawing some cider in the cellar, George heard God speaking very loudly to him and pressing him to keep his promise. George answered, "Yes, Lord, I will serve you, but I'm not ready yet."

HIS CONVERSION TOOK PLACE

in a very remarkable manner. He had moved from Connecticut to Philadelphia for the centennial exhibition (1876) and kept a boarding house. One of his boarders, Sam Pyne, disregarded the eighth commandment and got into the hands of the police, telling them he lived with George Washington. The police visited George and charged him with receiving stolen goods. Both men were sentenced to

SIX YEARS HARD LABOR.

George then many times thought of his past life and what a fool he had been. A fellow prisoner one day asked him to give his heart to God, and another lent him a book, but as he could not read this did not do him any good. At last he began to

PRAY IN EARNEST

and asked God to teach him to read the Bible. He learned to read God's Word and had no relish for any other book. He reports: "I then asked the authorities to allow me a spelling book so as to be able to learn my Bible faster. One day when the cell was quite dark and quiet, I saw a beautiful light shine into the cell, and heard angels singing, 'Glory to God in the highest!' and a voice said quite plainly, 'George, it is the Bible you must read,' repeating this twice over." This so impressed his mind that he never desired to read any other book, the Bible being his

CONSTANT COMPANION.

Since his conversion he has read it through several times. When this flood of light came into his cell he got so happy he shouted, "Glory to God" and sang a chorus. The jailer, not understanding what was the matter came and ordered him to keep quiet but George said, "How can I keep quiet when I am so happy? I am saved. Hallelujah!" After serving his full time in prison, he left behind him the character of being the

HAPPIEST MAN THAT WAS EVER THERE.

He removed to Danbury, Ct., and when The Salvation Army commenced meetings in that town soon was found at the meetings eagerly drinking in all that was said and done. He took part in the meetings and was

QUITE AT HOME

with them and has been ever since. As we listen to him we feel that God is speaking. When we look at his fine, manly frame, six foot high, with his bright intelligent face, and hear the burning words of love from his lips we thank God for a salvation that can make such a change. When Barnum's show visited Danbury, George was invited to go and see the procession but he said he could show the people something

MORE WONDERFUL THAN BARNUM'S ELEPHANTS.

He could show them a man that was once a slave, body and soul, but now was free. May God abundantly bless him and use him in the salvation of many souls, is the prayer of yours in the war.

Four

The Colonel and the Captain

Not long after Sam, now a Major in The Salvation Army, was commissioned as traveling evangelist, someone else demanded attention on the western seaboard. Newspapers carried no account; neither did the Salvation Army *War Cry;* still, Earl Edward Lord, born in March, 1901, to Edward Henry and Eliza Lord of Niagara Falls, New York, was destined to play an important part in the Brengle ministry, beginning his human adventure with an unusually robust squall.

A professional cook, Edward Lord died when Earl was two and his brother Delmar eight, leaving Eliza with a single determination: that her family would never "darken the door" of the county poorhouse. She put her sturdy Canadian-Irish trust in the God of her fathers and in order to support herself and her boys, took in washing, sewing and boarders. She sewed hooks and eyes on cards in a local factory, turned her hand to a variety of other jobs, not neglecting the womanly skills of home and garden, and the fine art of fishing. Eliza could uncannily haul in a catch when neighbors' lines went dangling. She taught her sons to work hard inside and outside home so that both became competent floor-scrubbers and expert cooks.

Delmar, six years older than Earl, left home at 17 for the beckoning west coast and soon, volunteering to drive one of the first Max Sennett Keystone Kops comedy patrol wagons, began what led to an illustrious career as a pioneer "talking picture" director. Husky little black-haired Earl absorbed Del's home duties, fretted about his mother, mimicked every vocal soloist he heard, and was baptized in the Baptist church, wondering what all that water signified. When he was nine, a neighbor who'd joined The Salvation Army asked if she could take him to afternoon Sunday school.

"Good way to keep him out of mischief," observed Eliza. "Go along, Earl."

"Ma!" Earl bounded into the cavernous kitchen at tea-time. "It's not like Sunday school at all. They got music!"

"Music," said Eliza. "What did you expect—a cemetery? God's house always has music."

"Not this kind!" said Earl. "They keep right on singing, and they clap their hands—and the piano keeps running up and down—and they have horns and a drum and—"

"Nonsense," said Eliza. "Not inside. It must have been a festival of some sort. Go do the dishes and set the table."

But *they* did sing with joy and much repetition, and there was an arpeggio pianist, and a brass band to inform God all was right with His world. What's more, one Sunday afternoon Earl trotted home with an ancient battered cornet bundled inside his jacket.

"Look, Ma!" He held it out like a jeweled coronet, whispering, "*Mine.*"

Earl learned the usual beginner tunes from The Salvation Army hymn-tune book: "Always Cheerful," "Joy in The Salvation Army," "Duke Street," etc., but two headliners in the Niagara Falls corps that became his favorites were "To the Uttermost He Saves" and "O Boundless Salvation." Soon, he begged to attend Army meetings "regular." After much consideration and prayer, Eliza fastened two foot-long hat pins in her faithful russet felt and hurried to Eighth and Orchard Streets.

"Captain," she told corps commanding officer Edmund Hoffman, "if it's good enough for my boy, it's good enough for me. We'll both join if you'll have us." And so it was, until she went to Glory 62 years later.

Earl couldn't imagine anybody have so much fun in church. He practiced hard, soon was made a uniformed bandsman, under the direction of Bandmaster George Pyke, learned to play a trombone and sang so melodiously that it wasn't long before he was singing in small groups and soon even by himself. During his teen years, he was strongly influenced by a 22-year-old corps assistant, Lieutenant Charles McNally.

"Ma! The lieutenant can do anything! Isn't he just great?"

"God is great," said Eliza tartly. "The lieutenant is a nice young man, Earl. God gave him gifts. He's sensible enough to develop them."

But fatherless young Earl thirstily observed the incomparable Charles McNally: dynamic, kind, excellent cornetist, sweet tenor soloist; exciting and persuasive preacher. Oh, to be like the lieutenant! Sometimes he told the lieutenant so, longingly, self-conscious of so many shortcomings.

"Oh, Earl, Earl," would be the reply, "you just don't know what God can do with boys." Then he'd tell about some wild escapade, concluding: "And *that boy* was Charlie McNally!" Earl always took heart at that and marched on.

In 1918, just after his 17th birthday, Earl entered the Salvation Army training College to be trained as a cadet for officership (ordination). The New York headquarters building which previously had housed the college had recently burned so the training period was unusually short, four months, and was conducted at the Men's Social Service Center (for alcoholic and other distressed men) in Philadelphia. Never having been separated from home before, Earl was scared and homesick. Who was he to think he could do what God wanted? He would be failing and failing and failing.

Doggedly he completed the prescribed course of lessons and listened to or at least sat through the necessary lectures. He earnestly participated in prayer meetings and street work. It was on the street the cadets spent most of their time: distributing collection boxes, selling *War Crys*, visiting needy people, praying with folk.

"Lieutenant Earl Edward Lord—out of Niagara Falls, New York—to assist in the command of Syracuse, New York." Commissioner William Peart read the appointment. Earl saluted. The Commissioner returned the salute. A new 17-year-old officer had been certified in the ministry of the "gunless army." Earl had vowed to obey all lawful officer orders and to carry out to the utmost of his power all orders and regulations of The Army. He had also promised to be an example of faithfulness to its principles, to advance to the utmost of his ability its operations and never allow, where he could prevent it, any injury to its interests or hindrance to its success. He had promised to maintain a strict personal discipline which required, among much more, abstinence from intoxicating liquor, baneful drugs, low or profane language, all impurity, including unclean conversation, the reading of any obscene book or paper, and the use of tobacco.

Further, he had promised not to allow himself any deceit or dishonesty, never to treat another in cruel, oppressive, or cowardly manner but to protect such from evil and danger so far as he could and to promote to the utmost of his ability their present welfare and eternal salvation.

Finally, he had promised to consecrate all of the time, strength, money, and influence he could to support and carry on the salvation war, believing that "the sure and only way to remedy all the evils in the world is by bringing men to submit themselves to the government of the Lord Jesus Christ."

Finally, he had promised to be a "true soldier of The Salvation Army" till his death.

Now to the battlefield to fight God's great war of love with never a faltering footstep! In the next two years Earl learned much about battling, and faltering, hurting and blurting out his resistance when his idea of proper spiritual tactics was neither understood nor appreciated. Music! Music! Music! His superiors regarded him as a singer, an instrumentalist when he longed to preach and teach and pray over sinners. Wasn't that what officership was all about? Christianity?

After four months in Syracuse, he was appointed to assist at Brooklyn; in six months he was sent to Harlem where he remained a year, growing more and more discouraged.

"I began to feel that all the Army offered me was a horn and songbook and I became restless, rebellious, and discouraged," said Earl later. "So I went home." After two months he was again in an appointment, this time in Newberg, New York, where he served almost a year, but again resented being starred as a musician. Home he went again, discouraged and disgraced in his own eyes.

"I can't take it, Ma," he confided and for three months fumed and criticized his leaders because he daren't criticize his Creator. Then came a letter from the territorial field secretary, Colonel Alexander Damon. "You are being considered as a secretary-singer for one of The Army's leading evangelists," read the letter. "Report to territorial headquarters at once."

But *that* was what all the fuss was about! He didn't want to sing and he didn't like detail! *Please, God, what is this all about?* prayed Earl. *Am I supposed to accept always exactly what I don't want?*

In New York, the gentle-visaged Damon told Earl, "It's a much coveted appointment, Captain. You are being considered as an aide to Colonel Brengle."

The *great* Brengle? Earl winced visibly.

"Colonel, I'm not—"

"We know something of your musical ability," Damon continued.

"And the rest can be learned. You're alert and quick, Lord. Can you type? Do you happen to know anything about shorthand?"

"Nothing. Nothing at all, Colonel."

Despite lack of training and obvious fear, Earl was enrolled in business college where he again became despondent about his lack of qualifications. He decided not to study any longer. Then came the 'phone call he would never forget. "You are ordered to report for an interview to the home of Colonel Samuel Logan Brengle, residing at Arlington, New Jersey."

"I shall never forget that experience," recalled Earl. "I was struck by the light that shone on his face. He was a handsome man, aquiline nose and kindly brown eyes, white softly curling hair and beard—but there was something more. I couldn't define it then—or now—but I felt as if he were giving me a gentle hug, though he never touched me."

"Welcome, Captain," Brengle said. "I'm so happy to see you. Come, we'll have a little chat."

Earl recounts:

He told me I'd been officially appointed to travel with him. He briefed me on the up-coming campaigns. He gave me specific instructions with regard to my responsibilities which entailed the purchase of railroad tickets, timetable, baggage arrangements and writing corps officers about the time of our arrival at the respective corps where we were to campaign. One of his requests was that I inform local corps commanders about a suitable hotel room where he could have ample sunshine and, as far as possible, quiet. He prayed with me, and I marched from his presence confidently—comforted and comfortable. That reassuring attitude seemed to be one of his greatest talents with his fellowmen.

The first campaign on which Earl accompanied "the beloved Colonel," was conducted in Bangor, Maine, in 1920, Earl was asked to sing in the first meeting. Returning to the hotel after the meeting, he was asked to report to the Colonel's room.

"Come in, Captain." Brengle's eyes twinkled; his manner was

not grave or foreboding but Earl remembered that "authority and priority were notable" as he later found they always were. "He pointed out some of my weaknesses on the platform. He stressed diction, poise, articulation, and choice of songs. He told me that he observed that I did not stand upright with shoulders back and chest high when singing. I assured him that I would do my best to improve, and, under his watchful and approving eye, I did."

Brengle was not a soloist but he did know music and knew much about voice development. In his graduation letter to son George he had expressed his usual interest in voice quality, counseling:

But I must say that one thing Mother wrote about was a disappointment to me. She said your voice was not so good as it was four years ago. Now, why should that be so? A young man of 21 ought to have a voice quite as good, if not considerably better, richer, stronger, purer than when he was a boy of 17. I don't like that and I hope you don't and that you will set to work to correct it at once.

1. You ought at once to begin to bathe your throat carefully with cold water every day.

2. Wear a loose low collar. I always do that and purposely, for the sake of my throat.

3. Exercise your neck and chest every day.

4. See some good teacher of elocution and get some few suitable exercises for your voice and practice them a few minutes every day. I have done this for yours, so that today my voice is one of my chief assets as a public speaker.

Please do all this for the sake of your Dad, if for no other reason. . . . Go to a good teacher and tell him you do not want him to train you to speak any given manner but you want him to tell you how to train your voice so that it will be the most perfect instrument it is possible for you to make it. And send me the bill. But remember all the teacher can do is to show you the way to do it. You must work it out yourself. You must practice, practice, practice. A few minutes a day will work wonders with your voice if you work on right principles. Do it.

For five years "The Colonel and the Captain" were almost continual comrades. Brengle grew to regard Earl as a son, patiently leading him toward spiritual maturity, never condemning when Earl failed, especially in his struggles with discouragement and disillusionment.

"My boy," he would say, "up and marching. Press the battle!" with a light pat on the shoulder and a pertinent prayer, would urge the single soldier in his immediate command to march on. "Life is a series of mountains, Captain. Climb with me! God made the mountains, and He made our legs. Climb with me. On! Up!"

"He had a penchant for mountains," Earl remembers, "and always felt he could climb any that came in his way. Though he was aging and his heart was quite bad during those years, still we often enjoyed the sport, and sometimes we had our picture taken atop one or another."

Though Brengle was not a musician, Earl noted that he knew exactly what he wanted in his meetings.

His choice of sacred songs was a *must*. I remember on one occasion I sang a song entitled, "In the Land where the Roses never Fade." That evening he called me to his room and said, "Captain Lord, I did not like the solo you sang in the meeting. Remember, we will never get souls converted if we just sing songs that have no message and no meaning here. Sing about Jesus, His love, His compassion, His love for the sinner, and when you do this, you will find a response in the heart of those who listen to your singing. Sing songs like "The Ninety and Nine," "At the Cross there's Room," "God's Trumpet is Sounding," and "I'll Follow Thee of Life the Giver."

Earl soon discovered that Brengle detested ostentation, including that of vocal soloists who "performed" in worship services. "I have sat with him in churches many times," remembers Earl, "and listened to some high-pitched soprano or tenor bursting their boilers to obtain volume and effect. He would turn and in a pained voice comment, 'Vocal gymnasts. No spirit.'"

Brengle also held a strong opinion regarding the use of talents dedicated to God. Earl remembers a campaign in Dallas, Texas:

I went down one day to the auditorium to do some vocalizing. I had with me some secular music which I rather liked and proceeded to accompany myself on the piano, singing, "The Road to Mandalay," "Stout Hearted Men," and "Invictus," and one or two other secular songs. I was in the middle of one of them when I suddenly felt a gentle tap on my shoulder and looking up, saw it was Brengle. He quoted kindly but firmly to me: "Take my voice and let me sing, always, only for my King." And I learned that, at least preceding spiritual efforts, the heart, hand, and head must be fully concentrated on the purpose of Kingdom building.

Earl watched and listened in wonder as he heard Brengle open the Scriptures and communicate a compelling message of Divine love to tens of thousands of people, great numbers of whom decided upon radically changed lives to be controlled by God.

Brengle's preaching, to Earl, was compelling not primarily because he knew and believed the Scriptures but because he was a living exemplar of what he preached and he always included himself in his considerations, often drawing from personal experience to emphasize his point. He knew that sorrow bowed many men tragically, and would often talk in this manner using such a Scripture reference as Rev. 21:4: "God shall wipe away all tears from their eyes and there shall be no more death, neither sorrow, nor crying, neither shall there be any more pain."

Looking straight into the eyes of his audience, for he used very few notes in later years, he would say something like:

From infancy my life has been punctuated by tragic losses, surprises, and pains. I do not remember my devout father. He made the soldier's sacrifice during the Civil war when I was a very little child, and my earliest recollections are of a bereaved and weeping girl-mother, sighing, sad-faced, and broken of heart.

In my adolescent boyhood when a young fellow most needs his mother, I was away from home at school where I received my first telegram. It read: "Come home. Come quickly. Mother is dying." When I reached home she was dead. At the beginning of my Salvation Army career, a Boston rough hurled a brick at my head and felled me with a blow that laid me out of the work for 18 months, and gave me a shock from which I have not wholly recovered in 35 years.

In the midst of my Army career I was stricken down with an agonizingly painful and dangerous sickness in a far-off foreign land, where I lay at death's door among strangers for weary weeks, returning home at last almost helpless, a mere shadow of a man. Some years later, lying helpless in a hospital, with a great surgical wound that threatened my life, word was brought to me that my sweet wife, the darling of my heart, was dying. . . . Oh it is easy to preach in full and robust health about 'grace, fathomless as the sea; grace enough for me,' but the test comes in proving and practicing it in danger, in broken health, in poverty, in loneliness and neglect and in sore trial:

> The toad beneath the harrow knows
> Precisely where each sharp tooth goes;
> The butterfly along the road
> Preaches contentment to the toad.

The rub will come to that butterfly when he too gets under the harrow. Can he preach contentment then? The value of testimony depends, after all, upon the degree and certainty of knowledge. I say to you then, lost? I have known that, but He found me. Guilty? Condemned? Undone? I have known that, and He forgave me. Unclean? I have known the impurity of my heart, but He cleansed me. Weak? Powerless? I have known that, but He has baptized me with His Holy Spirit, and power came into me. He came. Hallelujah! Poor? I have known dire poverty, been without a dollar, but He clothed and fed me. He said He would, and He did. Lonely? I have wandered with aching heart through the dark labyrinthine dungeons of loneliness and I found Him there, and was no more lonely. Perplexed, bewildered? I have been at my wit's end, but He was not at His. Fearful? Afraid? I have known nights of torturing fear, and then He has drawn nigh and said, "It is I; be not afraid," and all my fears have fled. . . .

God does not make pets of His people and especially of those whom He woos and wins into close fellowship with Himself, and fits and crowns for great service. His greatest servants have often been the greatest sufferers. They have gathered up in themselves and endured all the pains and woes, sorrows and agonies, fierce and cruel martyrdoms of humanity, and so have been able to minister to all its vast and pitiful needs, and comfort its voiceless sorrow. *God means no harm!* He assures us that "all things work together for good to them that love God." Then He leaves us free to believe and prove it and be at peace, or to doubt, repine and rebel and suffer needless woes of heart and mind piled on top of every affliction that may overtake us. Let us stir up our faith and sing:

> Since all that I meet shall work for my good,
> The bitter is sweet, the medicine is food;
> Though painful at present, 'twill cease before long,
> And then, o how pleasant the conqueror's song!

Though Brengle loved preaching and was continually preparing for it, there were times when he realized it was of secondary importance or even not needed. Such an occasion happened during a campaign in Grand Rapids, Michigan. One Sunday morning he leaned over to Earl on the platform and asked, "What are you going to sing this a.m., Captain?"

"'I'll Follow Thee, of Life the Giver,'" said Earl.

"I'm very tired this morning," continued Brengle. "My body aches and my mind is as dull as an oyster. Pray for me, Cap!" As usual, Earl was called on to sing just before the message. After one stanza and chorus there was a commotion at the rear of the auditorium and a voice cried out, "God, help me!" Then a young woman came running toward the penitent-form, weeping. She was followed by another, and another. Earl continued to sing, and before the song was finished, 12 people had knelt. Brengle never got to his feet that morning and was in good energy by evening, when revival broke out and a multitude of people decided for God.

Earl took Brengle's dictation, wrote most of his letters and articles and typed reams of manuscripts on the subject of holiness in preparation for publication in the United States and England. His letters were usually quite lengthy. He corresponded with people all over the world, officers of high and low positions and rank, to the humblest corps cadet in the smallest corps. He loved people, often referring to them as "the sheep for whom the Shepherd died." Quotations from the Scriptures were "part and parcel" of his letter writing, and, recalls Earl, "I assure you, it wasn't easy to translate Bible verses and put them on paper in the manner he wanted them to be. He always edited my work and made many, many corrections."

Attending Brengle in thousands of public services, Earl came to accept him as the most singular and exemplary person he had ever met. That Brengle believed God, His manifestation through Christ Jesus, the Bible, and in his fellow beings as precious to Divinity, Earl affirmed. However, closeness of proximity to such nobility did not, at that time, give Earl complete victory over his own inner turmoil. Still he fell prey to anger, frustration, rebelliousness, loneliness, and self-pity. *Perhaps,* he sometimes felt, *you had to be a Brengle to have a Brengle experience.*

"So simple, so simple," Brengle would say.

So difficult, so difficult, Earl would ponder.

To prepare himself for the preaching, indeed, for the day, Brengle spent at least an hour in private devotions with his Bible as his textbook, and every morning he would rise early and get down on his knees beside his bed to search the Scriptures for soul food to begin his day. He used a red pencil and marked verse upon verse that brought special revelation to him. Earl prizes Brengle's Bible, given to him on Christmas Day, 1924, and inscribed: "Presented to Captain Earl Lord by his affectionate old friend, fellow traveler and campaigner, Signed S. L. Brengle, Colonel."

After a devotional period he was ready for a light breakfast, usually a dish of shredded wheat and milk, and another day of correspondence, visitation, conferences, and preaching. Now sixty years of age, he attempted to include as much walking in his day as possible and was a firm believer in physical fitness. "He often admonished officers to look well after their bodies," remembers Earl, "cautioning them that they must be most careful of God's temple." This being before automobiles became so popular, he often expressed his belief that every officer should have at least four pairs of shoes so that they could change and rest their feet. He exercised daily, and found especially helpful sitting-up exercises that were done in bed in the early morning and other times when he rested. These included pulling his wealth of hair and beard. Only months before he died, youngsters in the St. Petersburg, Florida, corps, where he was wintering, were excited when they discovered him running around the town park circle in his gym shorts. He was careful regarding diet and exercise and benefited greatly from quietness, though he didn't often get it. Earl attributes Brengle's remarkable capacity for life to his spiritual virility. "He didn't have a remarkably strong body and had endured many illnesses and physical disabilities, most distressing of which was bleeding ulcers. But he was a remarkably happy person."

In Earl's estimation Brengle was never moody. He concentrated completely on the matter at hand, and always seemed to be enjoying himself. After a late night meeting, his pace would be a little slower as they walked to their hotel but he'd smile and say, "Praise the Lord! A blessed day tomorrow, Cap!" Also, he drew great enjoyment from conversation at which he was extraordinarily adept. Earl declares that "Brengle's conversation around the dinner table at home and on the field was something everybody enjoyed. He felt he could get closer to people in this way, always quoting Scripture and relating experiences he enjoyed in Christian service."

His sense of humor was spontaneous and childlike. The following is a fair example: Colonel Ralph T. Miller was whizzing along in a Model T. Ford in order to get Brengle to an engagement on time. "Slow down, Ralph! Slow down. I'd rather be Commissioner Brengle late, than the late Commissioner Brengle." And he enjoyed the simplest fun: late in life he was traveling to London by ship. There was to be a New Year's party hosted by the Captain. It had been a rough day, and a committee of younger officers decided a party was too fatiguing and perhaps inappropriate for the Commissioner, suggesting to him that he rest in his room during dinner.

"What?" cried Brengle. "And miss the party? Of course, I'm coming down—see you in the dining room!" And he was one of the most delighted party-goers, wearing his paper hat at a rakish angle and joining in full voice for "Auld Lang Syne."

Quotations, from himself and others, characterized his conversation:

I feel as well when I don't feel well as when I do feel well.

Don't get the cart of feeling before the horse of faith.

Don't change trains in a tunnel.

You can't prevent birds from flying around your head, but you don't have to let them build nests in your hair.

A stick that is about straight is crooked.

He cautioned young people:

If some of you listening to me tonight are not careful, the devil will give you a wife or a husband, and if he does, he will give you a hell of a life. Let the Christ who was present at the wedding of Cana give you your life's companion, and if you do, you will never regret it.

He also expressed an intriguing belief concerning war, strife, trial, and temptation: "The old Welch preacher believed that when these are present, *something of moment* is taking place in the spiritual world. Now, what do you think of that?"

He could be firm and official when occasion demanded, once telling Earl to "put your thinking cap on and keep it on," when Earl forgot to display books on a sale table and, "Don't let this happen again," when Earl found day-old mail stuffed in his tunic pocket. Another time: "Captain, do not take liberties, this is my personal endowment and should be respected," after Earl, in graceless familiarity, had leaned over and pulled his beard. He had dignity and a sense of proportion and fitness of the seriousness of life and God's calling, but balancing this was his remarkable good nature and sense of humor, both of which endeared him to the multitudes—and to Earl. He could tell some very witty stories. One of his best was about a young man who courted two ladies. One of them was beautiful and could cook to perfection whereas the other was very homely but had a beautiful singing voice. He finally married the homely one and waking to see her head upon his pillow the next morning, gasped, "For heaven's sake, sing!"

Though he drew adulation from throngs of people and was accustomed to compliments, he never felt complimented when people remarked, "Colonel, if I could just be like you what a happy life mine would be." He would answer, "I am what I am only by the grace of God and His Son Jesus. A sinner saved by precious Blood."

Brengle not only preached in Salvation Army halls and in churches but also to any other group which made a request. These included civic clubs, colleges and universities, high school assemblies, parent-teacher associations, service clubs, and women's groups. Kindly and sensitive to his audience, he nevertheless spoke truth as he perceived it and could not be diverted from a Bible basis. He preached salvation through Jesus Christ, and "the cleansed and victorious life" through the agency of the Holy Spirit for all who would fully commit themselves to God. Though superbly educated and enjoying a fluent vocabulary, Brengle had learned through the years the value of simplicity in speech as well as in other aspects of life. His "word lessons" and illustrations were both simple and powerful. Commenting on this, Brengle would often tell of an incident that happened when he was preaching in the days when Lily accompanied him. He used the word "decapitated." Behind him a firm voice said in a loud whisper, "Sam, tell them he cut off his head!" He declared he never again used a word which could not be understood by unlearned hearers.

Besides his public preaching and informal "at-home" conversational ministry there was his usual around-the-clock concern for others. He noticed all, everyone, about him and simply could not keep from speaking of the Lord of his life. If he talked to the elevator operator in a hotel, he would say, "Well, you have many ups and downs in this job, don't you?" and when the operator would say, "Yes," Brengle would use William Booth's classic reply, "Just make sure your last trip is up." If he were honored by a local leader, he found some way to mention God. Once he was chatting with the commander of the American Legion in St. Louis, Mo., in a high-rise building far above the city skyline. They studied the sky, mentioned the magnificent view, then Brengle said, "Are you a Christian?"

"No, I don't believe I am," said the man.

"Well now, would you like to be?"

"Yes," said the commander, and knelt down.

To an officer comrade, Major Glenn Ryan[1], who walked with him through a park as he spoke about God to a gardener, responding to the admission that "I wish I could speak so easily to people as you do," Brengle said, "It is not easy for me either, but when I know I must, I speak quickly."

One of the most charming incidents of his personal dealing concerns an all-night train ride. Brengle had to use the men's room, and there he found the porter shining passengers' shoes to the whir of the wheels. In between the lurch of the train and the rub of the shoebrush, Brengle said, "My brother, are you a Christian?"

"Nope," said the porter. "But my wife is."

"Not good enough," said Brengle and before he returned to his berth, he had tucked the porter into the comfort and security of divine love.

There is a captivating sequel to this story. First, soon after, the porter recounted his experience to a traveling Salvationist. "He

---

1. Later, Commissioner Glenn Ryan, Territorial Commander for the U.S.A. Southern Territory.

was an old gentleman in his pajamas. He knelt down there among the brushes and prayed for God to save my soul. And he must have come back again after I packed up, for this morning I found a little Gospel among my brushes. I've been reading that book, and I tell you, man, it's alive!"

Two years later, a Salvation Army girl was taking a long train ride to her mother's funeral. She was sobbing when a porter came and asked gently, "Do you know Colonel Brengle, ma'am?"

"Oh yes! All Salvationists know and love him."

"Not surprised. He prayed with me at midnight on the train. Please tell him I'm praying for him every day and Jesus is getting better and better in my soul." Her tears dried up as the porter comforted her.

Thus sped by five years of amazing activity for young Earl and his beloved Colonel. Victory! Victory! Victory! Occasionally, Brengle's step seemed to slow a little, especially after midnight as they trekked back to their hotel rooms. And he seldom ate much. His heart, troublesome for many years, sometimes stiffened him with pain, and his stomach or other troublesome "machinery" caused increasing distress. Infrequently, he mentioned one or another to Earl; more often, he did not, but Earl noticed that his color was not good, his face looked drawn. He could not preach as long as he wanted to. Then one night he came to Earl's room.

"Cap, I think I'm ill. I think I have got to see a doctor—now."

Earl called the local corps officer, who rushed Brengle to a local physician. After examining him, the doctor said, "Colonel Brengle, you must know the worst. You will die very soon. You have cancer."

Cancer? *Cancer.*

He called Earl to his room.

"Cap, the doctor says I have a malignancy. Well, if I have to go, I want to die in my own bed. We're going home."

APPENDIX

Brengle's Favorite Music

Brengle's favorite song may well have been "O Love that Will Not Let Me Go." It was sung at his funeral by Earl:

SB #536   TB #732

O Love that wilt not let me go,
I rest my weary soul in Thee;
I give Thee back the life I owe,
That in Thine ocean depths its flow
    May richer, fuller be.

O Light that followest all my way,
I yield my flickering torch to Thee;
My heart restores its borrowed ray,
That in Thy sunshine's blaze its day
    May brighter, fairer be.

O Joy that seekest me through pain,
I cannot close my heart to Thee;
I trace the rainbow through the rain
And feel the promise is not vain,
    That morn shall tearless be.

O Cross that liftest up my head,
I dare not ask to fly from Thee;
I lay in dust life's glory dead,
And from the ground there blossoms red
    Life that shall endless be.
                                        —George Matheson

Brengle loved the following songs especially:

            "How Sweet the Name of Jesus Sounds"
            "Take the Name of Jesus with You"
            "O Boundless Salvation"
            "There Is a Name I Love to Hear"
            "Rescue the Perishing"
            "Tell Me the Story of Jesus"
            "I'll Follow Thee of Life the Giver"
            "There Is a Green Hill Far Away"

"Wonderful Story of Love"
"Thou Christ of Burning, Cleansing Flame"
"Blessed Assurance, Jesus Is Mine"

These were the solos he most often requested Earl to sing:

"None of Self"
"Love Divine from Jesus Flowing"
"God's Trumpet Is Sounding"
"There's Pleasure in His Service"
"Take Time to be Holy"
"Into a Tent Where a Gypsy Boy Lay"
"Alone"
"The Ninety and Nine"
"They Bid Me Choose an Easier Path"

These were the choruses used most in the great "after" or prayer meetings which Brengle led:

Trust, I will trust;
On Jesus all my care is laid;
Trust, I will trust;
And I will not be afraid.

Into my heart, into my heart;
Come into my heart, Lord Jesus;
Come in I pray; come in to stay;
Come into my heart, Lord Jesus.

Have faith in God, the sun will shine
Though dark the clouds may be today;
His heart has planned your path and mine;
Have faith in God; have faith alway.

He's the Hearer of prayer and the Answerer too;
There's nothing too hard for my Father to do;
He lightens my care, brings joy everywhere,
Just to know that My Lord is the Hearer of prayer.

Give me a heart like Thine,
Give me a heart like Thine;
By Thy wonderful power,
By Thy grace every hour;
Give me a heart like Thine.

And yet He will thy sins forgive (repeat);
O come along, for Jesus is strong,
And He will thy sins forgive.

I'll follow Thee of life the Giver,
I'll follow Thee, suffering Redeemer,
I'll follow Thee, deny Thee never;
By Thy grace I'll follow Thee.

Keep in touch with Jesus,
Though your joy be dimmed;
Let no cloud nor shadow sever you from Him;
Joy or sorrow meet you,
Friend or foe you meet,
Keep in touch with Jesus;
He will keep you sweet.

I have not much to give Thee, Lord
For that great love that makes Thee mine;
I have not much to give Thee, Lord,
But all I have is Thine.

Five

Letters to a Very Young Captain

The Colonel and the Captain hurried home. As they embraced goodbye, both sensed that the great campaigning days together were over. It was the termination of almost 40 years of continual travel for Brengle, the prairie boy who wanted to make a name for himself, the impassioned husband who knew a lifetime of separation from his "little heart's ease," the acclaimed teacher-preacher who dared proclaim an unpopular, divisive message that influenced hundreds of thousands to cast a personal vote for God personally and sacrificially manifest.

Finished? thought Sam. *Finished at 64? Somehow, somewhere, there is more and better to follow. Praise God!*

National Headquarters was immediately notified, Salvationists and other Christians around the world began a vigil of prayer. Leading physicians were consulted and eventually a new diagnosis was made: Samuel Logan Brengle had a very sick heart and a much impaired excretory system; a long-suffered duodenal ulcer might quickly deteriorate to malignancy, and the least strain could end his earthly tour of duty.

There was no appointment ready for Earl so he was ordered

home to await one. As soon as Brengle was able to lift a pen he
wrote his beloved "boy," including details of his condition:

A lot of people write me, begging me not to die, telling me how much I am
still needed, just as if I were determined to die. Well, I'm not in a hurry,
unless the Lord wants me in some other world and has nothing more for
me to do in this. I hope still to carry on, and you must help me with your
prayers.

Thus, a sixteen-year fellowship continued, mostly by correspondence, until the "old friend and comrade" was, in Salvation
Army terminology, promoted to Glory. Most of the time Brengle
took the initiative, often concerned and disappointed regarding his
young friend who alternated gyroscopically between elation, loneliness, discouragement, disillusionment, intellectual inquiry and
sometimes spiritual progress and achievement. Often his "old
Colonel" perceived and sent an encouraging message, demanding
trust and industry from his "boy." Through the years Brengle's
physical condition gradually deteriorated to include deafness,
arthritis, and such impairment of vision that the enormous scrawl
and sprawl of his sentences made his writing almost unintelligible,
but he remained as vigorous and alert in spirit as when he'd first
begun to march. If Earl did not report regularly there would be a
postcard or a note such as this:

"How are you? I hope all is well. How is it in your soul? 'Keep thy
heart with all diligence for out of it are the issues of life.' 'Fight the
good fight of faith.' I pray for you, Earl. II Peter 1:1, 12." Another
time he wrote: "I wonder what dark deed I have done to cause me
to be so wholly forgotten and ignored? How are you? And how is
the work?"

After being visited by Earl, he would comment, "Come again!
The room and bed are at your service." The statement was typical
of his philosophy—all he was and possessed was "at the service" of
his fellowmen.

Encouragement was predominant in the letters, supported by a profusion of Scripture verses. Soon after their separation he wrote:

I think you are quite as gifted as he and God is just as ready to bless you. So I watch your career with fatherly interest and prayers. "As long as he sought the Lord, God made him to prosper." And so He will make you, if you seek Him diligently, day by day. Read Joshua 1:8, Psalm 1:2. God bless you, dear Earl, your affectionate old Colonel.

A few months later, he protested the fact that Earl had been promoted to the rank of Ensign (age 23) and had not so informed him:

When my son George was made a Captain in the U.S. Army . . . he wired me, for he knew I would be happy and when he was made a member of a leading law firm in New York, I think he wired me, for he knew I would be happy over his success, but my boy Earl ignores me and lets me learn of his promotion in a roundabout way. It isn't fair. Give me a square deal.

This continuing intensely personal interest, especially when Earl knew how massive was Brengle's correspondence, served as Gilbralter to an often rolling stone. If such a man as Brengle believed in him, how could he give up on himself?

After Earl was put in charge of his first command in West Chester, Pa., corps, Brengle's letters were not only more intimately filled with spiritual counsel, practical advice about corps work, officership, personal devotions and discipline and the deepest yearning and concerns of his spirit, but also he reprimanded when it seemed needed. In a sense, his letters through the years that followed became a manual for young officers, always supported by Scripture. That he meant every word, Earl never doubted. That his advice seemed difficult to accept, even impossible at 23 and 33 Earl never doubted. But that every word would be one day treasured in the velvet-lined treasure chest of his memory, he never even considered. Now, a 79-year-old veteran officer who often burdened his beloved "old Colonel," so often skidding and scuffling as he resisted submitting his will to those who did not seem to understand and appreciate him, Earl knows the tenderness of spirit that would occasion hallelujah tears from Brengle. Earl continues peacefully on his soldier road, still singing a Brengle campaign favorite: "My King's in the battle; He's calling for me. A salvation soldier for Jesus I'll be."[1]

Only a short time ago, a woman dying of cancer whom he and his wife Janet had loved and befriended during years of sorrow and pain, commented: "I don't understand Earl at all. He seems simply to live to help others. No fuss No bother. No burden. I think he must be a saint."

In 1925, life changed completely for both the Colonel and the Captain; recovering slowly Brengle wrote:

The Commander (Evangeline Booth) says no one wants me to retire, and the General writes me that he is not happy at the thought of my retiring and that he thinks a rest will enable me to go on. So he is changing my work so that I shall write more and do long, heavy campaigns less. I like the arrangement. Pray for me, Earl. Read Corinthians 15:57.

Soon he was writing not only more prolifically than ever but also was doing some traveling and preaching. Old articles and new were enclosed in book covers; old books were republished and new ones written, until two generations later, Samuel Logan Brengle is known almost entirely for his books. Busy as he was, if Earl didn't keep him informed he would write: "I am interested in everything you are doing and everything that concerns your corps. And the more you write me the greater pleasure you give me. . . . Don't

---

1. For some time, Earl has worked three days a week in the Salvation Army correctional services program in Miami, Florida, with drug addicts, alcoholics and misdemeanor cases. Since December of 1976, he has worked in the Army's program in which, at request of the State of Florida, all persons convicted of misdemeanors pass through the Army's special program of probation (for Dade County).

neglect me again like that. I feel you are my boy, and get hungry to hear from you."

Earl wrote that his mother was concerned about him being alone in a corps. Brengle answered in 1925:

> I am enclosing a note for your mother. She must not worry about you. You are no longer a boy. You have much experience. You know the Lord. You are His and she must trust you to Him and His providence.

The note to Earl's mother read:

> I'm glad you have had your boy. . . . You must trust him in the hands of the Lord, as Moses' mother trusted him in his little ark of bulrushes on the River Nile. God will go with Earl and guide and protect him and I am believing that God will greatly use him in the future. I shall miss him. He has been a great help to me, and he has always been willing and ready to do anything he could to help me.

To Brengle all of life was important, nothing and no one was unimportant, and he often made it clear to Earl that the answer to all was in God, and that complete victory was possible over any difficulty. No subject was taboo with him and troubled people wrote him on every subject without embarrassment. He was always forthright, though he could be brusque in his directness. And he knew how to reprimand a young man sometimes more interested in local sports than prayer meetings:

> I was interested in what you wrote me about. . . . He had some great meetings, and in New England the officers wanted him back again. . . . Now, Earl, he wrote me some time ago while in West Chester and surprised me by saying that when he reached the city no one met him, and that you had not advertised the meetings. Then he wrote me again confidentially and said you left him one night to fight alone while you went to a basketball game or something of the kind. It seemed to me unheard of that you should do such a thing. . . . Is it true, dear Earl? He did not rail against you. He seemed rather grieved and felt that your heart was not with him, and that you were more interested in outside people and affairs than in The Army and the work you are in West Chester to do. Write me and tell me just how you are and all the facts. Your old friend and comrade.

After that, counsel flowed continually to Earl in his first command appointment as he was faced with the usual concerns of public meetings, visitation, personal discipline, enticements from the "outside," problems which would nettle a much older man, and the hydra-headed monster of loneliness.

Of a married woman who occasionally attended meetings and was "running around" with a younger man, he stated emphatically: "Beware of her! If she is a lewd woman, you *must* keep her at arm's length. Be kind but most faithful with her soul. *Never see her alone.* Always have someone with you." As always, he concluded with encouragement:

You are just at the beginning of blessings. They will flow on through the years and broaden and deepen like a great river, if you keep seeking God diligently every day and keep in close step with Jesus. You know what it is to get discouraged, so you will know how to help the lieutenant (a recent appointee). Tell him to read Joshua 1:5 to 9 and Psalm 42:5 and 11, and 43:5.

Two lonesome boys together apparently could not strengthen each other sufficiently, for soon the lieutenant "left the field of battle" and Earl was again alone. He fell prey to discouragement again and again but Brengle would have none of his self-pity:

Too bad that you are alone, but you will know better how to feel for lonely people. There are many of them in the world and they need a ministry of comfort and cheer. Seek them out and cheer them up. Old people, widowers, and many a young man need fellowship, and just a bright cheery word from an understanding heart often illuminates a whole day or week. So learn the lesson hidden away in your loneliness and it will enrich your ministry to others. Stir your people up to look after the lonely ones . . . resolve to minister to lonely and lowly and hidden people.

That Brengle himself was not immune to the ache of loneliness was sometimes evidenced in his letters, a yearning that multiple hotel rooms, swift jostling trains, jerky buses and noisy streetcars intensified. In 1927, he wrote:

My dear Earl . . . wonderful meeting in Grand Rapids. . . . I wish I could hear you sing again as you did that morning and that we could have some more of those blessed meetings, but those days I guess are gone . . . and I must plod on alone. Your affectionate old Colonel, and your lonely old Commissioner.

Not long after, Earl's loneliness was focused specifically for he began to court, mostly by correspondence, Captain Janet Keeler, a young officer in command of the Detroit, Michigan, #5 corps. Immediately struck by her beauty both of form and spirit, her capable command of the Army platform and her delicacy of spirit, he determined that she would be his wife. Certainly such strong attraction meant God had ordained the union. He confided his belief and sense of urgency to his old Colonel, who replied:

So you think Janet Keeler is the girl, do you? I'm glad she writes you good letters. Respond with the very best that is in you. Then you will not only win her affection but also her deepest respect. Too often, young people in courting so behave that while they do not fall out, they do not highly respect each other and that means unhappiness later. . . . If I can help you in any way let me know. I want you to get happily married and shall feel almost as though I was getting married again myself when you do.

Janet Keeler was a competent, talented dedicated young woman. Her first corps appointment had been to assist Captain Eva Symmonds in the Alma, Michigan, corps. Captain Symmonds was the daughter of Mrs. Major Eliza Shirley Symmonds, who as a teenager started The Salvation Army in the United States. Here, Janet had been expertly trained and was soon made officer in charge of three thriving corps: Mt. Clemons, Detroit #5 and, Pontiac, Michigan. Before becoming an officer, Janet had been a proud, fashionable, rather worldly young beauty who had never quite been able to forget two profound events which God used powerfully in her life:

When she was three, according to her recollection, she had accompanied her parents, Canadians who now served as officers in the United States, to Montreal, to a "send-off" of delegates to the 1904 International Congress, her father traveling as solo cornetist ith the Canadian Staff Band. There little Janet got her first glimpse of the famed Evangeline Booth, then commander of the forces in Canada, as dressed in a scarlet robe and surrounded by children "of all nations," she conducted the farewell service. Tiny Janet was entranced and never forgot the song the children sang:

> I think when I read that sweet story of old,
> When Jesus was here among men,
> How He called little children, as lambs to
>   His fold,
> I should like to have been with them then!
> I wish that His hands had been placed on my head,
> That His arm had been thrown around me,
> And that I might have seen His kind look when He said,
> "Let the little ones come unto Me."
>
> —Jemima Lake

Janet grew up in a Salvation Army home[2] but felt no "call" to officership and resisted concerted attempts to make her "decide for the work," especially in the light of her parents' commitment. However, during her late teens, once again she came under the powerful ministry of Evangeline Booth, then National Commander of Salvation Army forces in the United States, and after a compelling address, she went to the penitent-form feeling only that inside her "something had to give." So long did she kneel, that her father, who as Divisional Music director was leading combined brass bands, sent a message: "Is there anything I can do, Jinkie?"

---

2. Daughter of Staff-Captain and Mrs. Robert Keeler, her mother being a pioneer of S.A. work in Canada, nee Maggie Ebsary; and her father a Salvation Army musician-composer, director, and cornet soloist. After the Ballington Booth schism, for some years he traveled as musician with Adjutant George Bennard, when the latter composed "The Old Rugged Cross." Janet is also sister of Colonel R. Lewis Keeler, for many years Central Territory *War Cry* editor and first national *War Cry* editor-in-chief; and of the author of "Peace Like A River."

She simply couldn't stop crying. Well-meaning persons angered her with their bombastic advice, and it was not until her quiet corps cadet guardian said simply, "Dear Janet, what are you going to do with your life?" that she made her decision. Now, queen bee in the busy hive of a successful corps, she was in no hurry either to fall in love or get married.

Earl continued to court by correspondence. Sometimes he forwarded Janet's letters to Brengle. The old mentor wrote:

I like Janet's letter. She is a sweet girl and I hope you may get her for your own. Write her out of the deepest and best things in your soul. Give her your testimony and your promise in every letter. That will encourage her to write the best that is in her. Cultivate and help each other's spiritual life and then if God does give her to you, you will understand and love each other all the more. Just keep the matter quietly before the Lord. Don't be anxious. I rather believe that she is the girl for you, and if so, God can give her to you.

Brengle was speaking from his own experience, remembering well how he had stated to God as a seminarian: "Lord, if You don't want me to be married, let me know. But if it is Your will, I have one request to make: help me find a woman who will love You supremely. Then I know she'll always love me. Choose for me."

In succeeding months Earl wrote Brengle of his yearning and impatience, mentioning the fact that Janet and he served in different territories. (The Salvation Army at that time kept lovers as far apart as possible to test their love.) Brengle wrote:

I don't know just how long you would have to wait to get married if you get engaged now, but as both you and Janet have been in the work for years I rather think you could be married by Christmas. [The Salvation Army required a waiting period for "courtship," meaning permission to correspond; next came engagement; and finally marriage.] I hope Janet is the girl. Is she going to Grand Rapids to talk over the possibility of engagement with her mother? If she writes me, I'll do all I can to help you . . . if you have a picture of her let me see it. If she is as good looking as her brother, she must be rather striking in appearance. . . .

About a month later, he questioned,

Have you heard from Janet? Don't be discouraged. "Faint heart ne'er won fair lady." If her mother objects, go and see her mother and press your suit. If she turns you down, pray and trust and try again. Above all, trust. God will give her to you if she is the right girl—if you quietly pray and trust.

In July, Brengle wrote happily:

I hear you have sent in an application for your engagement. Congratulations! I'm awfully happy about this. Tell her so. Write me a long letter and tell me all about yourself, your work, Captain Keeler, etc. I see she is farewelling. Where does she go? Chicago may not want to let you have her as she will be lost to the Territory, but in that case, Jenkins [under whom Earl had served], as National Secretary, can help you no doubt. Let me know if any hitch comes up. However, it may go through all smoothly.

All went well and the date was set for February 24, the old Colonel, of course, to perform the ceremony; however, circumstances intervened. Just before the marriage Brengle wrote:

God bless you, dear Earl, and fit you for the holy sacrament of marriage. It is a very sacred relationship into which you are entering. Janet is a splendid girl and you must reassure her and pray constantly for each other, seeking to work each other up in faith and devotion to the Lord Jesus and to the great work to which He has called you.

He further urged that they must develop all their gifts and make the most of every hour, and they would go far. Concluding that they must carefully and often read the F.O. book (*Orders and Regulations for Field Officers*), he concluded:

A girl like that should be an inspiration to any man. . . .
I pray your married life will be as altogether precious and helpful as was mine. Study Ephesians 5:21 to 33 and ask God to help you to live up to the standard set forth for the husband and you will then find wedded life an unmixed blessing. God bless you, dear Earl!

As he wrote he must have been remembering a small gold ring

and its inscription: *Holiness Unto The Lord,* a living-room filled with the whosoever, his immediate separation from his darling Lily as he crossed the ocean for cadet days, of the separations that followed, but also of a union that he firmly believed could never be broken.

In June of 1927, Earl wrote Brengle that a special joy was in store for them, and Brengle answered:

> I rejoice with you and Janet in the joy that is coming to you, I trust, with the little stranger that will soon be in your arms. Life will take on an entirely new aspect for you at that time. I know how you love little children, and once the little one begins to grow and smile at you, your heart will overflow as never before.

He then mentioned his daughter Elizabeth's baby:

> He is flourishing like a young bay tree, and is a little beauty, a honey pot, and sugar bowl, a jam dish and all things sweet and beautiful rolled in one! Keep close to Jesus! He is our Hope, our Peace, our Kinsman-Redeemer, and our surety for time and eternity. . . .

When baby Janet arrived, he wrote:

> Dear little Janet, I'm so glad you have come safely and I'm eager to see you. I love you already and feel almost as though I were your Grandpa. . . . I congratulate you on your Daddy and Mama. . . . You may find them a bit hard to manage . . . but they are nice people and you will love them when you have gotten better acquainted with them. You are new to this old world and they will have much to teach you. . . . bye and bye they will tell you all about the loving Heavenly Father and about the Lord Jesus, and I hope you may love God, believe on Jesus, and grow up to be strong, happy, and useful and help make a better world. God bless you, you darling little girl.

Little "Jinkie" was born at home, and due to inadequate post-natal care, Janet ailed. Being busy with corps and family life delayed the necessary corrective surgery for several years. Her health began to deteriorate.

"Get Janet off the building into a more quiet place if possible," wrote Brengle. "Tell her to have at least two seasons each day in which she lies down for a bit and rests. And give her a cup of hot Ovaltine at night. Sleep in twin beds for a while."

Janet's health remained poor. Soon the Lords were appointed to Cleveland and then Canton, Ohio, where a thriving corps kept them breathless, with band, songsters, youth groups, more than 300 in Sunday school, and in emergency lodge—with woodpile— for it was now the depression days of 1930. Janet became very ill:

I cannot see that you have made an irregular or unreasonable request to be allowed three months in which to nurse Janet back to health—you must get her health restored, if possible, and at once, else she will become a lifelong invalid. Don't be discouraged, trust God and keep a brave heart. Tell Janet to look up and trust the Lord. She must not be discouraged. Bless her!

At this time Earl learned that Brengle included the stewardship of money in his philosophy. Frugal as he was regarding himself, eating and dressing simply, caring little for the usual recreations and amusements, he often noted that care and concern about worldly possessions often marred life. Earl struggled financially and received this letter in 1934:

I herewith enclose a check of $100 which I trust you may be able to repay at $5 a month. The depression has hit me somewhat along with everybody else, and I have been carrying a heavy burden for other folks who were hopelessly prostrated financially. It looks as though I shall have but little left by the time financial recovery returns; however, the Lord has been good to me, and I am glad to be able to help others.

Noting the tragedy of one-time comrades who had left Salvation Army ranks and whom Earl was attempting to re-interest, he wrote:

I note what you say about. . . . I know them very well and was very sorry when they left the work. I think probably the friction that exists between them and . . . is due to money matters. They watch each other very closely to see whether the mother is going to give more money to one than the other. It's another case of money getting into the hearts of people and crowding out brotherly love and the Christlike spirit.

He kept no accounts receivable record, and often seemed to sense need. He wrote in 1935: "Are you in any immediate need of money for personal necessities?" Twice, Earl borrowed sums from him. Brengle's letters of acknowledgment were revealing and amusing:

"Dear Earl, Is this the right sum? It cost a little more to telegraph it, but I suspected you were up against something," and later, "Thank you for the P.O. order. I'm trusting you to keep the account. Don't pay more than you get. I have no idea how the account stands and forget all about it till you remind me." A bit later: "Thank you for the five but please don't think that there is any hurry in paying me. Take your own time." And in 1936, just before his death: "Thank you, dear Earl, for the money order. It is quite all right to send it when it is convenient for you. I hope you are keeping track of how much it is. I am not."

Though his letters were always cheerful, and he insisted on being active, Brengle was continually plagued with physical distress. He had another serious seizure in March, 1928, and wrote:

Thank you for your very lovely letter of March 6. I am so glad to know that you and Janet are praying for me. My surgeon wants me to come to the hospital. He says that the condition I have is liable to degenerate into cancer and become hopeless if not attended to in time. I am not alarmed at all, and I would much rather not have the operation, but I think I am in very good condition for it, and he says if done now we shall be taking it in time, and I shall have no more trouble. Just pray that the Lord will guide us all, and fit the surgeon for a clean-cut job. I want to go to 80 if I can.

However, he had been called to preach and preach he would. Not long after the operation he wrote: "I spoke briefly to Dr. Cadman's[3]

---

3. S. Parkes Cadman, long-time pastor of Park Avenue Church in New York City.

church Sunday morning. He said I must come preach for him twice next January and asked for dates. I hope to go. I'm getting stronger. My chest no longer distresses me as it did. But just now I have an attack of rheumatism in my foot and this interferes with pleasant and rapid locomotion. See Psalm 103."

Gradually, Brengle was weakening. By 1932, he knew times of great physical distress, noting on April 29:

Dear Earl, I'm over here at the National Holiness convention. I preach today and Sunday morning. I'm not very strong. My heart is seriously weakened and the specialist says I must take great care or I may drop most any time. So that is that. But bless the Lord anyway! I've lived longer than the average and God has blessed and blessed me. See Ephesians 3:20–21.

After a setback when 75, he reported:

I'm nearly 75 and I do not rally promptly from a physical setback. But hallelujah! I've had my day and God may leave me here a bit longer. I'm content.

Brengle believed in maintaining as strong a body as possible; he well understood the energy that public life and involvement in the lives of others demanded. He believed strongly in physical culture, daily exercise and care in diet. He jogged daily until weeks before his death and did exercises, some of which could be done even when bedridden. Of the death of a comrade officer, he wrote:

Yes, it was a great shock to hear about . . . death. He was 19 years younger than I and ought to have sung at my funeral, but I spoke at a memorial service for him at St. Petersburg. He was a dear fellow, and he ought to have lived into his seventies as his father did. I am afraid he helped to dig his grave with his teeth. He was not always discreet in his eating. He had diabetes and heart trouble, and if he had been careful as to his diet, as every diabetic patient must be, he might have been living today. He had been attached to New York headquarters for many years, was always singing and a friend to everybody.

Janet's health continued to be poor, an operation was performed and many attempts to re-invigorate her were tried, but her body remained weak and was a source of discouragement to both Earl and her. In response to a letter from her in June, 1933, Brengle wrote:

Dear Janet, during the night I was thinking of Paul's trials, his thorn in the flesh, infirmities, reproaches, necessities, persecutions, and distresses, and how he gloried in them because they were an open door into the sufficiency of the grace of Christ. They were Christ's opportunity to reveal to Paul the fullness of His love and grace and strength, and Paul's opportunity to display to the world the patience and peace and unconquerable faith and tender love Jesus gives to the devoted and trusting soul.

Then I thought of you and prayed that you too may prove His grace sufficient. This time of trial and weakness may be the one time through eternity granted to you for just this display of His grace in your life. You have the "infirmities," "necessities," "distresses," but Paul was ahead of you, for added to these he had "persecutions," and "reproaches." I have had all but the persecutions. Maybe I have had them, too, but if so, they hit me so lightly that I cannot remember them.

Read II Cor. 12:9, 10 and see how Paul triumphed. Also, Romans 8:28 to 39 and II Cor. 4:17, 19. I have been helped, too, by Isaiah 63:9. It is comforting to think that in our affliction our Lord is afflicted—He sympathizes and suffers with us just as we suffer in spirit when we see our children or those we love in sorrow and suffering. God bless you, dear Janet!

In later letters he sympathized:

I hope Janet may improve but she must make haste slowly and just be patient. I know how hard it is to be patient and give nature a chance to knit up the ravels of a tired and broken body. She has youth on her side. If she were ten or 20 years older it would take more time. So tell her to thank God, be cheerful, look for the gold and silver lining of every cloud, and to trust and not be afraid.

And to Janet, mentioning his own declining health,

I know how to sympathize with you. Well, we must learn to suffer patiently and hopefully. God will not give us new bodies in this world, but

He may renew and patch up the old ones, and then some day we shall have new ones, not made with hands, eternal in the heavens. Bless God!

In the midst of the heat of battle, the Lords' tiny Jinkie suffered a debilitating illness. Brengle wrote:

Dear Earl, I am very sorry to hear of sweet little Jinkie's illness. I know your anxiety, and I pray for you and Janet and her. George had pneumonia when he was a little fellow and then Elizabeth was paralyzed, and for years was in an almost helpless condition. So I know how to sympathize with you. And the dear Lord knows, too. One of the tenderest texts in the Bible is this: "He is touched with the feeling of our infirmities." And again, "He was moved with compassion for them."

This is grief, but you will be taught through it to minister more understandingly and tenderly to other fathers and mothers whose hearts are torn with anguish. May the dear Lord comfort you and Janet and lay His healing hand on the sweet little girlie.

He continued his consolation to Janet:

Don't be discouraged about your health, dear girl. Just be careful and rest patiently in the Lord and let big husky Earl and the band boys and a fine lot of locals do the outside work. You can be the inspiration in the home that Mrs. Brengle was to me. She was frail, but oh, what an inspiration. She was my heart's ease and I felt the lift of her prayer all around the world and the warmth and wealth of her love was like breezes from Heaven to me.

APPENDIX

Brengle gave Earl his Bible as a Christmas gift in 1924. He had hand-written therein the following inscription and quotations:

Presented to Captain Earl Lord by his affectionate old friend and fellow traveler and campaigner. For three of the four years I have had this Bible we have traveled and worked and prayed and read and wept and rejoiced together. From the Atlantic to the Pacific, from the Mexican border to Canada, we have sought souls together and in every place God has given us victory. Make this Book your daily study and live by its truths and you will be more than a conqueror. Joshua 1:7 to 9. I Tim. 4:12–16. II Tim. 3:10. Acts 20:32. Rom. 15:13. Jude 20 to 25. Eph. 3:14 to 21.

When as a babe I smiled and wept   time slept;
When as a child I laughed and leapt   time crept;
When as a youth I dreamed and talked   time walked;
Then I became a full grown man   time ran;
As older still I daily grew   time flew;
Soon I shall find in traveling on   time gone.
O Christ, wilt Thou have saved me then?   Amen!

I know Thee, Savior, who Thou art,
Jesus the feeble sinner's friend;
Nor wilt Thou with the night depart
But stay and love me to the end:
Thy mercies never shall remove;
Thy nature and Thy name is love.

'Tis Love! Tis Love! Thou diedst for me!
I hear Thy whisper in my heart;
The morning breaks, the shadows flee;
Pure universal love Thou art:
To me, to all, Thy mercies move;
Thy nature and Thy name is Love.

Christianity has three points: God, man, and his brother. One hand goes up to God, the other must go out to our brother. If I am tempted, I must look both ways, and consider my brother as well as my God. If I only look to myself, God, I might spend more money on myself, and drink wine, and ride my bicycle Sunday afternoons, for in themselves, these things may not be sinful, but when I look at my brothers, some poor, some weak, some worldly, I hesitate. The law of liberty would let me as I look up, but not the law of love as I look out.

No man shall place a limit in Thy strength;
Such triumphs as no mortal ever gained
May yet be thine if thou wilt but believe
In my Creator and Myself;
At length some feet will tread all heights now unattained.
Why not thine own?
Press on!
Achieve! Achieve!

Said the robin to the sparrow,
"I should really like to know
Why these anxious human beings
Rush about and worry so."
Said the sparrow to the robin,
"Friend, I think that it must be
That they have no Heavenly Father
Such as cares for you and me."

The sweet persuasion of His voice
Respects the sanctity of will;
He giveth day: Thou hast thy choice
To walk in darkness still.

The laws of nature are the habits of God.

I have one passion; it is He, only He!

One who spends his time trying to explain away hell and the unquenchable
fire, and the worm that dieth not, it not a penitent man.

Standing before the tomb of Jesus in Jerusalem, General Grant bowed his
head and said: "Here slept the real warrior. He conquered the world by His
love."

I walked a mile with pleasure,
She chattered all the way;
But I was none the wiser
For all she had to say.

I walked a mile with sorrow,
And not a word said she;
But oh the things I learned of her
As sorrow walked with me.

Lose the day loitering;
'Twill be the same story;
Tomorrow and the next more dilatory;
For indecision brings its own delays,
And days are lost, lamenting
Over lost days.

Are you in earnest?
Seize this very minute,
What you do or think you can,
Begin it!
Only engage,
And then the mind grows heated,
Begin it,
And the work will be completed.

Six

Battlefield Suggestions

Brengle was interested in all people, but if one Salvationist group drew him more than others it was corps officers—men and women "in the thick of the fray." Serving in a number of appointments as corps officers, Earl and Janet knew the usual challenges, victories, and failures, and all was communicated to their "old comrade and friend." He answered in the only way he could: with genuine interest, honesty, and love. Naturally, his special interests were stressed. As much devoted to the written as the spoken word, he often counseled regarding recorded thought and the publication of it. In 1934 he wrote:

My dear Earl,

I got the Christmas *War Cry* day before yesterday and immediately read Janet's article. It's splendid and touched me to tears. She has a gift. Tell her I said she must not bury the talent but use it, "Put it out at usury." It is not easy to write, at least not for me. I sweat and agonize over about everything I write, but when it is written and published and goes on its way to bless others, then my heart bursts with song. It is much like a mother's agony in childbirth, I suppose, only it's mental and spiritual. When the child is born the mother forgets the agony and rejoices over the child. So I rejoice and so will Janet, if she continues to write. She need not write long articles every time. Short little articles will be read and often carry the biggest blessing. . . .

Janet sometimes sent him poems such as the following:

> I smiled and nodded brightly
> To people that I knew;
> How could they guess
> My heart's distress,
> The sorrow in it too?
>
> I trotted by them briskly
> With footsteps firm and strong;
> How could they know
> My will to go—
> Just barely crept along?
>
> So as I hide my sorrows,
> Dear Lord, help me to see
> There are those
> Who too hide woes
> And need *my* sympathy.
>
>   —Janet

Months before his death, Brengle wrote Janet:

You can write dear Janet. Just let your heart move you and write as it does. When Jinkie is away at school, give yourself up to meditation, ask the Lord to help you and He will and in this way you may be used more widely than if you were in meetings every night. Don't think that you are useless, dear Janet. . . . Don't try to write long things. Don't weary yourself unduly, but begin. . . . Stir up the gift of God within. Read your Bible and get books and when an idea comes to you, jot it down and you will find little articles and poems growing in your mind—they are living things.

Creative writing was important to Brengle, judging from his clippings, though he seldom contributed to the field himself, and the writing he urged Earl to do, the over-busy, eager, self-demanding young officer, was quite other. If you are a noun-verb, subject-predicate person, then write that way, cautioned Brengle. Whatever came naturally and was polished to a gleam to glorify God, that record. It might be the very thing someone else is needing. He wrote Earl:

Why don't you do a little writing, Earl? Don't think you have to write something elaborate. The first thing I wrote for the *Cry* was when I was a Cadet in England in 1887. It was only about ¼ of a column but it caught the eye of Bramwell Booth and he said to my sister-in-law, Susie Swift, who was then editor of *All the World*: "That's the kind of writing we want in the Army." It was about a bad woman's first real love, the woman who washed the feet of Jesus with her tears and wiped them with her hair. A number of my articles in those early days were very short. The important thing is to write out of your heart and under the inspiration of the Spirit and with perfect simplicity, not thinking at all about what the big folk will think of your articles, but only what good you may do. I believe you could write. Try your hand at it some time and then if long after I have gone Home you feel like writing about me you can do so.

Brengle began to contribute to the *War Cry* and other Salvation Army periodicals when he joined the ranks, but it was not until his head was crushed by the thrown brick in Boston about two years later that he composed his first series of articles on holy living for *War Cry* readers. A few years later, during a period of great distress in the United States, when Commander and Mrs. Ballington Booth left the ranks and near chaos resulted, that the same articles were republished in book form, resulting in a profound influence that helped sustain Salvationists and set a tone of spirituality for coming years. However, it was not until 1925, when his appointment emphasized writing that many of his longer works were published.

Brengle often declared that public speaking was much easier for him than writing. For instance, in February of 1925, he wrote Earl:

"Thank you for your letter. I have delayed answering it because I am so very weak, and it wearies me almost to the point of pain to use my arm in writing. . . ." Yet, three months later he confided, "I have been working on a new book which I think may do good when I am resting beneath the daisies. . . . Pray that it may be so. My old heart which has been awfully dull, is beginning to function again. I wrote an article for the *Staff Review* this past week, 'The Mystic,

Wondrous Universe in My Backyard.' I don't know whether or not they will publish it but I hope so."

He had no special affinity for the typewriter and thus wrote out much of his work in longhand, an arduous process: "My dear Earl, I'm neglecting the typewriter. It's slow for me. I need much practice and feel I shall never develop speed." Near Christmas of the same year, 1924, he reported, "I'm sending you a copy of my new book, *Resurrection Life and Power,* which is just off the press. It will come a bit late for Christmas, but in time for the New Year. And may all that life and power be yours. Ephesians 1:2 to 4, 18, 20."

He was pleased with the book's good reception, especially when orders came from outside the ranks. In 1931 he noted: "A new book of mine is just off the press in London. . . . They write me that they expect a big sale and that outside religious papers are reviewing it." And when Clarence Hall's biography was published in 1932, he commented happily: "Mabee told me the other day he had just read Hall's story of my life. He thinks no one inside or outside the Army could have done better." After retirement and still yearning for his regular preaching ministry, though valuing the opportunity to write, Brengle again admitted his stress during writing: "London wants me to write . . . though writing is the worst thing that I do. It tires me all over, while preaching if not to excess is good for me."

So earnest was his belief in personal holiness, that he never hesitated to recommend his own books for use in teaching. In February, 1935, he wrote:

My dear Earl, may I make a suggestion, that you get about 25 copies of my little book, *The Way of Holiness,* paper covered. If you buy that number they will let you have them for less than 10 cents a piece. Give or sell them to your soldiers, ask them to read the book and get all the blessing they can out of it and then at the next soldiers' meeting let them tell what blessing they got out of it. The officer at the Bowery did that two–three years ago and said she had the most wonderful soldiers' meetings she had ever known.

Then you might get copies of that little paper, abridged edition of *When the Holy Ghost has come*. You can get that at the same price . . . and you might have your soldiers read that and report. Then you might get the paper edition of *Helps to Holiness*. I think you would then have them indoctrinated and it will help to build them up in the faith.

When he was unexpectedly promoted to the rank of Commissioner, after the age of retirement, he wrote:

Thank you for your congratulations on my new dignity. It came to me as an utter surprise. I never dreamed of such a thing. The writing that has brought this recognition to me was altogether a work of love and love never thinks about what it can get but only about what it can give. One of the joys of my life has been to give myself, my money, my time and labor without the least thought of reward.

Of the many subjects Brengle wrote about to Earl, only spiritual maturity was talked about more than the every-day work of the corps. To Brengle the corps was The Army, and soul-winning the single aim. All his life centered on winning men and women and children to Christ Jesus, believing that all else concerning a man will be righted when the great union is made. His correspondence is filled with practical and earnest advice, pleas, and commendation. Concerning Earl's first corps command in West Chester, Pa., in 1925, he began:

You are certainly getting a good running start in your new corps, with all these invitations to sing and play your instrument. You say you have "spent most of my time visiting among businessmen and ministers." That's good! Do you pray with them? Do you remember my story of Holgreave? The Captain who built the hall and died in bed? You remember how he prayed in his study and how it blessed him. Now, you do that. It will be a cross at first, but it will bless both you and the preachers and it will please Jesus and you will feel His presence very near as you do this.

Then he added, in epilogue fashion, as he often did, his strongest point last:

Don't fail to visit among the poor too, and let them know you are there to minister and bless them. They are the people who *need* you and that you can make into soldiers. Oh, that you may have a big blazing revival! Pray and believe and work at this and stir your people, however few and feeble they are, to help you bring this about. . . .

Always he steered toward the one great goal: "Don't let these outside functions wean you from The Army, but make them all bend to the one great end for which God has called you and for which you are in West Chester. I think you are going to have a mighty time there. I'm praying for you."

In a later letter he continued on the subject of visitation: "Visit the people but always take the lieutenant along where there are women . . ." and again,

Avoid all occasions for gossip. When out visiting, enquire about their souls, about their children, about their health, then read a promise, pray, and go on. Never stay in a house more than 10 or 15 minutes. Don't appear to be rushing but say what you have to say and be gone. Many officers spoil their visitation by staying too long. They will come to the hall if you interest them. When you visit, always mark a promise in their Bible before you leave and tell them to meditate upon it. Get the young people to bring their Bibles to the meeting and mark promises for them. Teach them to pray also.

Another time:

That is a good idea to send postcards to converts. When a soldier or convert fails to come to the meeting drop him a note and tell him you missed him but that you hope to see him in the next meeting. Follow them up! *Follow them up!*

He was wary of an officer's spending too much time with affluent Army friends who did not seem needy spiritually. In 1926, he wrote:

Don't spend too much time singing for or with outside people. Do a little of it but devote yourself to your own concern and your own people.

They are "the flock over which the Holy Spirit has made you overseer." Feed them. Visit them. Love them. Shepherd them. That is your business and nobody else can do it while you are there. Your future depends on your faithfulness to your own work. *Be faithful.* Give yourself wholly to it and God will bless you. The people will love you and your leaders will approve you, and your own conscience will commend you.

In recommending prayer daily for soldiers and converts, he suggested:

Ask the Lord to show you the way you can best help them. Carry them on your heart. Love them. Pity them their mental and spiritual inadequacies. And seek in all ways to fit yourself to shepherd and feed them. They are the lambs and sheep of Jesus. And what a privilege is yours. The fact that three D.C.s are trying to get you indicates that you are in demand, but just go on studying, preparing, praying, working hard, loving the people, getting souls saved and all will be well.

Brengle was ever eager to make the attraction of the Gospel visible and beautiful. He wanted clean and colorful halls, plain but enticing. There must be banners waving, colorful ones that shouted out the great glad news. Banner corps needed to have posters and placards, marching brass bands and bayonets of prayer readied. Anything, everything must be used to attract the seeker to enter God's house.

In 1935, he wrote to Earl:

Thank you for the two little papers from Dr. Batholow's Bible class. I am glad you are getting into touch with him. He will be a very good man for you to study. He will give you a lot of ideas and I think he will bless your soul. You will get points on how to build up a corps. Why couldn't you have a little corps paper of some kind? Of course, he has hundreds of members to whom to send his paper, but a little weekly paper full of points for your soldiers might tremendously interest them. Appoint two or three of the young people as reporters to report all the doings of the corps and soldiers and young people and the visitors. It will be something new and give them something to talk about and think about.

One time he suggested certain small but important details:

I was most happy to hear of the blessed times you are having in your corps. It is too bad that your hall is so unsuitable for your work. I hope you may get a good hall in the fall. Have you a bulletin board outside your hall, in which you put up the pictorial section of the *War Cry,* with invitations? There are a lot of little attractions that can be put up around a hall inside and out, that help to draw people. One or two electric fans in a hall at this time of year will prove a benediction. Some of your advisory board members or rich friends ought to give you a couple. Special prayer will help. God answers prayer still, but there is altogether too little praying these days. Go into your hall every morning for a half hour or an hour, and tell Him what you want for the day, and bring before Him the names of the sinners you are seeking to save, and ask Him to fill your heart with love for sinners, and *He will do it.* Take the F.O. book, which is the greatest book ever published on soul saving outside the Bible and yet is sadly neglected, and read what William Booth says about reaching souls and loving them.

Brengle loved children and believed that they could be attracted and won permanently to God at a very early age. Often, in his mind, they were the kernel from which a whole corps could grow. In May of 1925, just after Earl had been put in command of West Chester, he wrote:

Set yourself by prayer and thought and work to win 25 children out of that block around the corps building. Get the boys. Take them on a hike. Roast weenies and marshmallows with them. Start a band among them and go to Dr. Williamson for money to buy instruments. When anybody tells you that The Army is not needed in West Chester (as had been said earlier) tell them of the block with its 100 churchless children and ask them for a donation to help you win them. Get all the children and you will get the parents. God will help you. Keep on believing, praying, working, and you shall see the Glory of God.

In June of 1925, he wrote:

My dear Earl, are your crowds increasing? Are you capturing any more young people? Try and capture that 100 children in that one block. Get up some special scheme to get them. Why not start a girls' timbrel band, "The

Sam and Lily Brengle, 1914

Brengle's grandson,
Logan Brengle Reed.

"The Colonel and the Captain"
enjoy a mountain climbing
expedition.

Silhouette
from "The War Cry."

Janet Keeler Lord, 1924

Commissioner Brengle
and Captain Earl Lord
in St. Petersberg, Florida

Brengle at home for a brief rest.

Miriams," or like the Swedes, have a guitar and mandolin brigade? Your brains are young and more nimble than mine, and you will find some way to reach them. But don't feel that they are really reached until they become earnest, praying boys and girls.

In 1927, Earl had evidently written about a particular struggle, when the youths became active and aggressive spiritually and some older folk became jealous. Brengle commented:

I rejoice to know that your young people's work is so bright, but it is sad that the old folks have been so cranky and cantankerous. Sometimes it's well if people will not get right, just to let them slip out. If they are not right they can have the same effect upon a corps as the cancer has upon the human body, but you must still pray for them, that God may restore them and bring them back to their senses and to the corps.

Jubilant over the successes in the Canton, Ohio, corps in 1931, where there now was a Sunday school attendance of 325 and the hall was nightly "packed out," Earl wrote enthusiastically and received this reply:

You certainly are pushing things, Earl. I congratulate you on your wonderful Christmas distribution and upon the splendid corps you have. Why don't you open an outpost and overwhelm East Liverpool? Aren't there any places for outposts in Canton and haven't you two or three energetic soldiers who would grow with leaps and bounds if they had a responsibility placed upon them such as an outpost would entail? Give them something to do!

Were you with me in Wichita, Kansas a few years ago when Calhoun opened an outpost and gathered in a host of children and bye and bye made a corps of them? Then he opened another outpost and did the same thing, and he just about led the country. He went to Tulsa, Oklahoma, and he hadn't been there but a little while when he opened an outpost and when I was there we dedicated a beautiful new hall, had it crowded to the doors and shortly after that was a new corps. Go on, my lad! Set your soldiers to work!

Brengle understood teenagers and lamented when they were mishandled and lost to the ranks, particularly when through harsh disciplinary action, though he believed in sterner soldier discipline than did many other leaders. Band boys often came under special attack in pioneer days, often severing soldiership because of cigarette smoking (abstinence is part of soldier commitment for self-discipline) or lack of attendance at "open-air" meetings. He wrote in 1935:

I am very much interested in what you tell me about the corps, and especially about the band boys. I know what a difficult situation they make for you. Our band boys are one of our greatest assets, and at the same time one of our greatest dangers. I am writing an article on our band, and the importance of making it into a revival brigade. Let me suggest that you invite each band boy, one at a time or two or three in a group to come out and have tea with you, and tell them about your anxieties, your hopes, your fears, for them. Tell them you want their help.

Make each boy feel that you particularly want his aid, and that he can be a great help to you, or a hindrance, and urge him to give his heart to the Lord, and be God's man. Point out to him what a future he may have, and how in his youth he can plant seeds of carelessness, thoughtlessness, indifference, and sin, that will greatly hinder his future, and maybe mar and ruin it forever. Tell him he's at the seed-sowing time and the harvest of the future will spring from the seed he is sowing. Get the older soldiers interested in the band boys and ask them to speak to them one by one, not to preach to them too much but to enfold them in their prayers, their love, their sympathy. Get the young people's secretaries interested in them. Tell the bandmaster what you are doing and make it a matter of much prayer. And God will help you. I can't write more now, for in a few hours I'm off to the train. God bless you, dear Earl!

One specialty of his campaign meetings that he never ceased to use and to see great results from was a combined meeting, carefully seating the children in front. He described it in this manner:

I shall be glad to speak to the Methodist Sunday school Sunday morning and maybe you can get Roberts to do the Holiness meeting. I think it would tax me to do the two meetings. I am anxious to reach your children in the afternoon, and remember my old notice for that meeting? It includes all children from six to sixty-six with the sixes in the front and the sixty-sixes in the rear. Tell the people to come. We hope to have a wonderful time and we will do the meeting at night and I hope you shall see the Glory of the Lord and the saving and sanctifying of souls.

Prayer and Bible were inseparable to Brengle. God through the Lord Jesus Christ—that was his message. And to keep the soul fed and lively it must have both prayer and the Bible. Neither stood alone in his mind. The Bible was *food*, and prayer was deep meaningful conversation with the Almighty Presence. Thus, he considered of supreme importance in the building and thriving of any corps, the prayer meeting, Bible class, and soldiers' meeting. Life was one in the body of Christ—arms and legs, eyes and tongue never could function by themselves. Any amputation was not only painful but a disaster. A proper relationship with God, complete trust in Him—these made up the *summum bonum* for the prophet from the prairie. A year before his death, he said of his own personal prayer:

I have been getting up very early of late and praying. I was up before four o'clock this morning and had a rich time in my soul. I went back to bed, however, and had a little nap before finally getting up. I love to seek the Lord early in the morning. I get more blessing out of it than at any other time of the day. God bless and bless you, dear Earl.

Daughter Elizabeth mentions that in his last months on earth, he would often come downstairs, his face glowing, to report, "I've just had the most wonderful chat with Moses, Abraham, and Elijah!" or other of his long-time intimates.

He wrote concerning one of Earl's growing Bible classes:

The Lord bless you and guide you in the development of your Bible class. I think you are wise to introduce it in connection with your soldiers' meeting. When I was a Captain and had my soldiers' meeting, I dealt with any business that we had on hand very promptly, and then we had a Bible reading and a red-hot prayer meeting, and the soldiers got so blessed that outsiders used to beg to be allowed to come in, and sometimes we would let them in. Prepare especially for your Bible reading very carefully and prayerfully, and have your soldiers bring their Bibles with pencils and mark the passages of Scripture that you study, and in doing this the soldiers will be fed and their souls refreshed, and I hope you will see them grow. . . .

Special prayer periods were recommended by Brengle. He advised in this manner:

I rejoice over the souls you are having. That was splendid to have eight last Sunday night, and that you are getting young married couples interested. In Africa some earnest souls wanted to win a heathen tribe to Jesus so they started prayer meetings *at midnight* and prayed till morning and soon they had a revival on their hands and 50 new raw heathens were converted.

Continually he gave specific directions concerning Earl's own personal Bible reading, such as:

My dear Earl, let me exhort you to read over and over again and again Paul's two little Epistles to Timothy, meditate upon them verse by verse. Pray them with the very texture of your soul. Commit them to memory. You can commit a verse or two each morning while you are shaving. Do it and feel yourself growing in grace and divine knowledge.

Follow up the marginal references and you will become wise in the ways of things of God and become an officer equal to your job. When you have read those two Epistles over again and again until they are a part of your mental and spiritual life, then read Peter's two epistles in the same way and master them and let them master you. And then train your soldiers to read and read in the same way. . . .

Brengle agreed with Bramwell Booth regarding sermon preparation: "Prepare as if you never prayed and then pray as if you never prepared."

Soul-saving consumed him. The Kingdom of Christ Jesus on earth was the reason God had raised The Salvation Army; this was the central purpose of the Christian. Think it! Pray it! Study it! Act it! Particularly did he advise young officers: "Study what the F.O. (*Orders and Regulations for Field Officers*) says about soul-winning." His methods were old ones, simple ones. He believed that the "full salvation" of the leader was imperative. Next, food: study of Scripture and prayer, the student meeting his Teacher in learning and thanksgiving. Then came the preparation of spirit, mind, and body by active exercise of what had been acquired. *Then* ministration. And finally, *ad*-ministration, which was co-equal "in power and glory" but never to be sought for prestige-power purposes, or personal experience would stagnate and corporate ministry suffer staggering damage.

There must be both indoor and outdoor meetings, much visitation, soldiers' meetings and other "drills," often experimental, and every conceivable method used to attract and hold interest. Even so, nothing was as important as the consciousness of and submission to God's living, personal Spirit. Brengle believed that when people fell in love with God, they not only triumphed over self and were changed from dismayed, cranky, troublesome, sinning beings into singing, joyful Christians, but also that they developed a sense of responsibility for the well-being of others. Finally, it was always to be remembered that it was God who set His servants on fire, not gimmicks, or music, or group participation or social welfare or anything else—not even use of the Bible. The living Presence of the Eternal was the Attracter, Saviour, Ennobler, Empowerer.

Of the desire to win others to Christ, he wrote:

I can't tell you how happy it makes me to know·that you love to preach and have a passion for saving souls. Cultivate the passion and pray for wisdom and power to win them and doors will open before you as they have opened before me. The man of wisdom and grace, flaming with love for Christ and souls, will always find larger fields waiting him and people wanting him. Our people make a great mistake who are always panting after and scheming for some secretarial (headquarters leadership) position. The man most in demand of whom the people never get weary is the wise preacher who feeds the soldiers and wins sinners to Jesus. Study more and more to do that, dear Earl, and you will never grow stale or out-of-date.

In Brengle's mind the presentation of God's message must be

simple, direct, and alive with the preacher's own experience. It did not, however, need to be particularly *short*. If the speaker had world-shaking matters to present, and he held the interest of his listeners, he could justifiably speak for 45 minutes or an hour. After all, what was this brief time compared to that given any other chosen interest? Especially did he not want to hinder the prayer of the "after" portion of the service by ill-considered termination—or extension. People should have time to meditate on the message, be "warned" by carefully chosen songs and choruses and the earnest specific prayer of believers. All should be slanted toward the one who did not know God. Just before a serious operation he wrote, not of himself, but of the way to conclude Sunday evening meetings:

I do hope you are having a blessed time with Envoy Waggoner. It is not always easy after you have preached to pull in your own net, and probably he has not learned the art. A man is weary by the time he gets through his address ordinarily. Just as he pulls in the net, the devil is liable to attack his faith, and he needs help. You must take hold. You know my plan. I say to the folks: "The one we want to come is the one to whom God has spoken. There is someone here who knows God has spoken to Him through the message. You know that God has spoken to you, and He has spoken to you kindly. Now, come to the penitent-form!" Have courage, press the battle, and God will give you souls. I wish I could come down and help you. . . . I have considerable writing ahead of me, and I want to get that off. I want to get some articles read as I cannot do them while in the hospital.

Though interest in corps work was always personal and practical, the preponderance of his thought was still expressed regarding Earl himself. Often he mentioned Earl's singing, concerned with results: "I was happy that Damon put you up to sing. I think he will do more of that and you must select the best songs . . . the most spiritual ones, and be careful to keep well within the compass of the range of your voice, neither getting those that are too high or too low. Within your own range you have a marvelously musical voice." Again, this time regarding his retirement meetings: "Be sure and get the right pitch for your resonant baritone. I want that. It may not come till the officers' meeting Monday afternoon. I'm not sure of the program but be ready. I want *only the old Army songs*. The new ones seldom reach my heart. Affectionately, your old side partner."

The "old songs" were simple and specific. They extolled Christ Jesus, His saving grace, the wonder-working power of the Holy Spirit, the love and omnipotence of the Father. That is what Brengle forever hungered and thirsted after. Nothing, no one else. He wrote of this:

Your testimony that you have no other ambition in life but to fulfill God's will and win precious souls for His Kingdom greatly rejoices me and I am delighted to hear what splendid success you have been having. That record of over one hundred souls while you have been in Canton gladdens my heart. I hope you are turning them into soldiers and training them and disciplining them in a way that will make them soldiers for life.

Training and discipline, especially that of the self, were paramount to Brengle, and he often expressed himself thus:

Do all you can to develop the lieutenant. You can help to mature him. Let that be your aim. Give the boy every chance you can, urge him to cultivate all the power he has. Make him take the lesson once in a while, giving him notice in advance, but tell him to be praying and preparing himself, so that if he should be called on suddenly he will be ready. Make him help you to get out the reports, so he will learn how to do it. Above all, help him to be a holy lad. God bless you, dear Earl. I am mightily interested in you. Your affectionate old Colonel. I Corinthians 15:57, 58. Victory!

Brengle not only believed that exercise made one skillful but also that a person assimilates his concentration. In his mind, we not only become like that which we love but gradually, in *fact*, we are what we eat—spiritually, mentally, physically. If a man feeds on God, he becomes, in finite fashion, what Jesus promised: first, "servant," then "friend," then a little Jesus. Awesome, yet admissible. Did not Jesus say to his beloved disciples (Matthew 14:19–20): "Because I live, ye shall live also. At that day ye shall know that I am

in my Father, and ye in me, and I in you." How this experience could
be maintained in the life of a busy young Salvation Army officer,
Brengle was concerned about and often wrote Earl concerning his
conclusions:

. . . I would suggest that you pray, dig into your Bible for an hour, at
least a full half hour every morning before breakfast. Then in the forenoon,
do your correspondence and have an hour of study and reading of some
good book. In the afternoon, visit the people. Get your time systematized.
Don't let it fritter away. Hold yourself to a close program as far as possible
and you will find yourself "growing in favor with God and with man"
(Luke 2:52).

Have an hour alone with God each day and have Lt. Clark take an hour,
if you cannot take it all at once, take it in two half-hour periods. Take time
to be holy, and give God time to talk to you, mould you, teach you. . . .

Be sure and have the hour of earnest prayer and Bible study every day
and your own soul will become like a watered garden. We have to work at
our own hearts first and keep them with all diligence, then work for others
becomes easy and a joy. So live in West Chester that when you leave you
can say to the people, "I am free from the blood of your souls. I have lived
and done my best for you." Your affectionate old Colonel. P.S. Read John's
epistle *on your knees!*

Brengle considered the conservation of time important and was
an early riser. He believed that young Christians could well benefit
from a shorter period in bed. Often he cautioned Earl:

My dear Earl, it's an early hour, but I'm wide awake and while praying, I
saw you and wanted to be of some spiritual help to you. I feel that you are
my boy, and I long to see you strong in the Lord and full of His joy and
peace. You can be, Earl, if you give yourself wholly to Him and wholly up to
the work of winning and binding men and women, boys and girls to Him.
When you wake up in the morning, give yourself a good stretch, bounce
out of bed quickly, do some vigorous gymnastics, have a quick cold bath,
and then to your Bible and your knees with joy for a half hour or an hour.
If you make this a habit of your life, you will grow in your soul and in your
mind and your splendid body will become the vigorous and efficient slave
and instrument of mind and soul.

Take time to be holy. Meet God early in the day. Plan your work early in the day and then work your plan with all your might and some time I shall hope to come and spend a few days with you and Janet and the baby, and have some blessed meetings with you.

In another letter he mentions that 5:30 a.m. is a good time to arise for devotions, adding that Earl should employ "a notebook to take down any thoughts and directions God gives you." "At least once a week pray for each soldier, young and old, by name. Ask the Lord to show you the needs and the way you can best help them. Carry them on your heart. Love them. Pity them. They are the lambs and sheep of Jesus. Read I Thess. 2 and Acts 20:17 to 35; also John 21:15 to 17. Stick to your knees!"

Another time, the notebook was suggested for other than prayer periods: "Carry around a notebook with you and put down ideas, illustrations and Scripture verses that are helpful and you will find yourself very well equipped for your work."

Sometimes Earl tended to self-pity concerning lack of higher formal education. Never a believer in regret for the past, Brengle would counsel: "Now, don't you worry about not having had a college education. Read, think, bring to remembrance! Keep a hot heart, follow Jesus wholly and with joy and you will go further than 95 out of every hundred college-bred men. Bless you! You are a joy to me and I love you!"

Earl and Janet were appointed and re-appointed, to larger and larger, more demanding corps. Increasing visible success but also more demands, more problems, heart-breaking defeats. At times Earl resisted administrative decisions and restrictions and requirements. At first "the old Colonel" sought to make the way smooth with only positive advice such as, in 1935:

. . . I wish to particularly point out these portions of Scripture to you in this, probably the most important command you have had. See Acts 6:4. Read also Acts 20:17 to 35. Also read I Timothy 4:12 to 16. You will notice that this portion is addressed particularly to a young officer, Paul's adjutant,

Timothy. Ponder these words, meditate upon them, and ask God to help you pattern your life by them. Read I Cor. 4:9 to 13 and note the patience and the glad submission of Paul under trial, also II Corinthians 6:1 to 10, also II Cor. 11:19 to 29.

Difficulties began to multiply. Janet did not get well. There was insufficient leadership. Some of the soldiers quarreled. Brengle wrote reassuringly:

Dear Earl, I am sorry to hear that the corps has some members that don't like each other. Why don't you preach my sermon, or have you forgotten it, on "Follow peace with all men and holiness without which no man shall see the Lord." Give them two or three of my old illustrations and let them meditate upon it. Read to them John 15:7–17. Read to them my text in I Thess. 3:12–13, and read that searching word of Jesus in John 13 where He says: "A new commandment I give unto you, that ye love one another as I have loved you . . . by this shall all men know ye are my disciples if you have love one to another." And that word of John: "He that hateth his brother is a murderer." If hatred is in the heart, murder is there. We are to love even the unlovable.

In a fatherly but firm manner he continued, marking out what he considered to be a weakness:

Your tendency, dear Earl, I fear is to become a bit impatient, and if you are not very careful you may become critical and cranky under the trials you are subject to, and you may begin to blame people, but God may be permitting these for the discipline and training of your spirit to make you like Christ, who "when he was reviled, reviled not again and when he suffered he threatened not, but committed himself to Him that judges rightly" (I Peter 2:22 and 23). I commend especially to you to read Lamentations 3:25 to 27. That portion of Scripture was a great blessing to me in my young manhood and early officership when I was sorely tried with extreme poverty, with a frail little wife and a paralyzed baby. . . .

Earl and Janet were re-appointed, this time to a smaller corps and a situation which was not inviting. Downhearted at first, Earl nevertheless plunged "into the fray" and soon reported good results. Brengle was overjoyed:

My dear Earl, bless your heart! What an altogether good letter you wrote me! What a glorious word it was that woke you up that morning . . . quite worthwhile "coming down" from one city to another just to get the victory over the devil, but to win a lot of souls put the final touch to the victory. God is with you, my boy, and He is training you for larger and larger service, whether it be in large or little field of labor. I have often been made doubly glad by finding myself in some small difficult corner for there I could see God at work. If all our people could see this they'd stop itching for some enlarged field of labor and be happy and mightily used of God. It is not larger fields we need but larger hearts and a faith and more burning love.

We ourselves need to be larger men and then we need have no fear about larger fruitage in our work. A mighty crop of souls can come from a small field of labor if we do faithful work and water it with our tears. You are on the right lines and I'm happy as can be. . . .

Often he concluded such a letter with something like this: "And don't forget you have Janet by your side. She's a whole team in herself!"

Brengle remained consistently himself through trouble, torture, and triumph, and especially when Earl seemed to be wasting Kingdom-building time on self-recrimination or regret for past failures, his mighty spirit seemed to rise like a much-weathered ship, leaping over instead of sailing through the stormiest waves. He would write:

My dear Earl, God bless you, my boy! Forget the past and with face front, breast forward, live in the present for the future. Remember Paul's text: Phil. 3:13, 14: "This one thing I do, forgetting those things which are behind and reaching forth unto those things which are before, I press toward the mark for the prize of the high calling in Christ Jesus." Hallelujah!

As always, Bible verses were his final exclamation points: "Read Phil. 12:2 to 11, Jude 20 to 25, Isaiah 41:10 and Jeremiah 31:3; 33:3."

APPENDIX

The Secret of Brengle's Faithfulness to The Salvation Army

During the last years of his life, Commissioner Samuel Logan Brengle was asked to comment on a question raised by a former colleague and student friend, who told a Salvationist during a train ride that they had been collegians at the same college and that he had heard so much about the great man through his professors. He said he was personally very curious to know just why Brengle chose The Salvation Army when he had such bright prospects and what he supposed to be a greater field of usefulness, especially educationally. The man concluded with this question: "What did Brengle see in The Salvation Army to hold him all these years?" Brengle was asked to comment, and he did:

I saw hardship, poverty, brickbats, abuse, the scorn of the proud, the ridicule of the thoughtless, the contempt of many professing Christians awaiting me. These things I saw and found. But also I saw the Cross of Jesus "going on before."

I saw the lost sheep for whom the Saviour died, the sinners unreached and unsought by the churches. I saw Salvationists struggling and suffering to win these, and so I became a Salvationist. Later, I saw how ill-equipped were many officers and soldiers for the great task. I saw the Founder (William Booth) and our leaders burdened with overwhelming administrative duties and unable to reach our poor people and struggling officers on the farflung battlelines, and so I prayed and preached and wrote and set myself with full purpose of heart to feed the lambs and sheep of Jesus.

Evermore when at secret prayer and in communion with my Lord I heard His question, "Lovest thou Me?" and I answered, "Yea, Lord, Thou knowest I love Thee." His words would ring in my heart, "Feed my lambs—feed my sheep." And when sore tempted to leave the Army and seek an easier way and preach to a larger audience and more cultured than the few poor people who came to our little halls, I would reply to the tempter, "Who then will feed these sheep if I forsake them?" And I felt I could die for them rather than leave them. Little did I then see the world-wide ministry awaiting me. All I wanted was to be a servant of the servants of Jesus.

Seven

Last Days

Though Brengle's body wore almost completely out before his promotion to Glory, his "Hallelujah!" spirit remained, and his mind was unimpaired. He met with shrewd and loving consideration whatever life brought. In 1928, just before his retirement, he was a member of the high council especially convened to deliberate regarding the ill health of General Bramwell Booth. The proceedings attracted world notice, much of it critical when the council voted to retire the beloved leader. Brengle, an old and close friend of Bramwell, was sent with the sad decision in company with Commissioner Yamamuro of Japan. Of the experience he wrote to Earl in June of 1929: "Yes, we had a great time at the meetings . . . but a painful time at the High Council. I loved Bramwell Booth, but I had to vote for his retirement. I saw him, and he was an utterly broken man, wholly unfit for the superhuman task of a General. I believe God led us in our voting."

Nor was he reluctant in voicing his opinion to others as beloved: his own family, including Earl, with whom he often dealt sternly regarding temptation and defeat. Several times Earl considered leaving the ranks, through discouragement over Janet's health, tormented by greener pastures, a sense of ill-treatment by superior officers, or so he judged. He worked hard, saw results but had a natural resistance to orders he did not understand or that seemed ill-timed, despite acceptance of William Booth's edict: "The strength of The Army is built on two words: *love* and *obedience.*"

Earl's "old Colonel" well understood his tempestuous nature and had from the beginning sought to stabilize Earl, often perceiving trouble and not waiting to be asked for advice, writing such letters as this one:

Are you in any trial or trouble that makes you hesitate to write me? I fear so. But if so, do you not think that is all the more reason why you should write me? Have I ever failed you? Has not God given me to you as a friend to help you with your spiritual battles? I hope you are having victory but if not, fight through till you have and let me help you if you think I can.

Remember, it is thrice overcome that develops spiritual strength, gives knowledge and insight and fits you to help others. So "fight the good fight of faith, be strong and of a good courage . . . be strong in the Lord!" Bounce out of bed in the morning when you awake and set yourself to commit the Sermon on the Mount to memory (Matthew V, VI, VII). Don't lie abed and yield to any sort of mental, spiritual, or physical temptation. Stir yourself and fight the foes of your soul—gloomy discouragement, mental laziness, physical desire, spiritual sloth; and God will help you. He will shine upon you and put a shout and a song in your mouth.

Though he had left appointments without permission several times, Earl had never resigned; however, in 1935 circumstances combined to make him feel the world was against him. Conflict with a superior officer set him writing a letter of despair on the eve of planned resignation. Brengle fired back this reply:

I can understand what a trial this is to you, but dear Earl, trials are permitted to come to us for two reasons: first, to correct us when we ourselves have gone astray. Now, how far this may be the case with you, I cannot say. God knows. Second, to test your faith, your patience, your love, your steadfast endurance. God proves us in this way. Job lost everything but he held fast and God gave him double. Joseph was evilly and unjustly and wickedly treated by his brethren, and for years he suffered "until the Word of the Lord tried him" (Psalm 105:17–22). See also the story of Joseph in Genesis. It was in this way that the Lord was preparing Joseph for the highest honors, the greatest dignity, and the most amazing usefulness. So David himself was tried and persecuted and his life sought for 13 years by King Saul, but these trials fitted him to become the immortal Psalmist and one of the great rulers of all time.

Now, it may be that God is using this trial to prove you. Don't spend time blaming . . . or anybody else but do as the Bible tells you to: "count it all joy when you fall into divers temptations," or trials. See James 1:2 to 4. See also Romans 5:1 to 5, and Romans 8:28 to 39. You can very easily spoil God's wonderful purpose if you spend your time blaming men instead of joyfully and humbly seeking to know all God's mind in the matter and letting the trial work out its greatest discipline in your faith and patience, forbearance, and love. You are an Army boy. You are under vows to The Army. The Army has given you many opportunities and it offers you many more. Many soldiers and officers love you and they will grieve if you go and get out under these circumstances. Don't be rash but go on and dark days will emerge into bright days, and no telling what the next thirty years may bring to you.

I would suggest that you and Janet pray much about it. Read Psalm 37:1 to 6. Go over your consecration afresh and renew it and resolve to GO ON. And then I think it would be wise for you to get your doctor's certificate saying that Janet should stay out of meetings for three months or more if necessary until she has recovered, and then go and have a talk with . . . and lay the whole matter before him and explain to him and the soldiers that Janet is going to remain at home and keep quiet for three months and you are going to assume all responsibility for the corps together with the soldiers. They will then understand that she is not shirking. If you do this joyfully, cheerfully, forgetting about your experience with . . . you will find your sky brightening. The soldiers will rally to your help and God will pour out His spirit upon you and smile upon your labors and your peace will flow like a river and your righteousness as the waves of the sea.

You say you have contracted three evangelists. It is just possible you might do well with them financially, if you go out, and again you may not. You will have to furnish a home for Janet and Jinkie, and you will be away from them for long periods of time, but, doing as I advise you, you will be with them and the home will be provided for them. I have had trials myself in The Army and I write out of a wide experience and wise observation and in tenderest love for you. My old eyes are very poor (noting his illegible script). I will try to see you and talk this matter over. Be strong and of a good courage.

So far as finance is concerned: I had four or five dollars to eight dollars a week to live on when I knew that some were not friendly toward me. I nestled down into the will of God, kept patient, believing for better days, kept on loving everybody, practicing holiness, testifying to the blessing, and God did not fail me. Blessed be His holy Name! And He will not fail you if you daily seek His face, bear patiently the trials of life and go on faithfully with your work.

There was a very large scrawled note in the margin: "Eyes very bad. Can't read and can't write . . . only believe!"

A little later, there was a hastily written note marked, "October 16, 1935—IN BED":

My dear Earl,

I'm deeply concerned about you. Don't make a mistake! If men treat us badly, God prepares special blessings for us, if we bear it patiently and meekly. Matthew 10:11, 12; I Peter 4:12 to 16; Psalm 37:1 to 5.

I think your trouble has two sides, and I dare not hastily judge headquarters without hearing what they have to say, and the regulations under which they act. But if there is only one side—your side—still I feel you should quiet down, trust God, and go on in love and faith. God will meet you on that road with blessings bigger than you ask or think. If you go your own way, you may miss Him altogether. I held on in Danbury without Mrs. Brengle—held on with the big Negro, the little hunch-backed girl and the lame lieutenant, while Mrs. Brengle was bearing George. You have a fine corps, fine band, full salary, and a good home. I had none of these, but I held on and God blessed and I would not for a million dollars exchange places with my dear boy George (a Brengle soloist who had resigned Army officership and had become a well-known evangelist).

Stay where you are! Pray for. . . . Fulfill your vows. Trust God. Rejoice in Him, and let Janet stay quietly at home during the winter, reading her Bible, praying for you as Mrs. Brengle prayed for me, and cheered me on. You will get the victory and God will give you souls and open doors for you in His own way and time. I'm far from well but I go on. Hallelujah! Love from your affectionate old Colonel.

The Lords did not resign. Instead, they served for another thirty years in a variety of appointments, retiring as General Secretary in the largest division in the great southland.

Though Brengle's life, writings, and preaching epitomized simplicity, and from the beginning he was determined to emphasize only the essentials of man's salvation, this does not mean that he kept himself from complex theological thought. For example, letters in Earl's possession note an exchange with Dr. S. Parkes Cadman, pastor of the New York Park Avenue Church, and in the 20's and 30's president of the Federal Council of Churches of Christ in America. Brengle had several times preached in his church, and they had both a scholarly and spiritual friendship. In 1928, in consideration of the evils of the day as they both saw them, Brengle suggested a nationwide "Family Day," similar to Mother's Day, to be set apart by churches for the nationwide consideration of the claims of the family. "Both directly and indirectly, the family is being attacked and undermined," said Brengle. "Has there been such an orgy of divorce since the days of ancient Rome as we are now witnessing in America? And however much the man and woman involved may suffer, the blow falls heaviest upon the children. That this tragedy is heartrending, I conclude from nationwide observation."

Cadman was happy to consider the suggestion, presenting it on his weekly radio program. He also shared thoughts regarding evil and the devil, another subject Brengle had commented on, listening to a listener's query when ill one Sunday morning. Brengle wrote:

Did you sidestep a bit in your answer to the question, "Do you believe in a personal devil?" My very old friend and teacher, Dr. Daniel Steele, whom you may have known through his books, *Love Enthroned, Milestone Papers*, etc. used to tell us that as the pure in heart see "God," so the pure in heart and only those can distinguish the devil from the workings of their own minds. This corresponds with my own experience, following that wondrous day when God purified my heart by faith and anointed me with the Holy Spirit. I found myself in a new realm of temptation and was as conscious of a spiritual presence tempting me as I was of a sacred divine Presence reassuring and delivering me. God bless you!

Cadman replied:

As you know, the doctrine of the personal satan is exceedingly involved. For myself, I lean toward it and believe that all such influence must have somewhere a personal source. But I do not believe in the doctrine which makes the world a divided empire between God and the devil. It is my faith that God is supreme and that all things must eventually work into unity for His will. I therefore take comfort in St. John's teaching that evil is a darkness which enhances the Divine Light and will presently pass away.

To that Brengle replied:

We do not seem to be far apart in our thoughts about a personal devil. I am sure there are men who are deliberately sinister, who take "pleasure in unrighteousness," do not hesitate to ensnare runaway souls, and it seems to me to be revealed in the Scriptures and to be perfectly reasonable to suppose that there are disembodied spirits as truly sinister. And it is a subject concerning which I dare not think or speak lightly. If it is a fact, it is a very serious fact, and you speak of what you term "the holy mystery of evil," a mystery which can only be explained upon the ground that its presence in life is intended to develop man's spiritual nature by resistance to temptation.

I can conceive what we often term *evil* as existing without sin, but I cannot conceive *sin* as existing without evil, and a personal devil seems to me to be related to the mystery of sin. . . . It was his failure to recognize sin that made John Fiske's book, *Through Nature up to Nature's God* so mystifying to me. He seemed to me to be wholly unconscious of sin, as I remember the book. He dealt with evil and made plain by some medieval monkish illustrations its beneficent character, but that left the terrible problem of sin untouched.

On the other hand I am not satisfied with the extreme view of Harold Alexander Whyte concerning sin. He seemed to think sin invincible, at least in this world. He confuses temptation with sin. Jesus died for sinners, bless His Name! And His blood cleanses from all sin those who, penitent and believing, walk in the light as He is in the light. How He will in the end deal with finally impenitent sinners, I leave to Him. Since He has allowed sin to begin I see no logical reason why He should not permit it to continue. It is an awful thing to contemplate. My friend and theological classmate, Dr. Charles E. Jefferson, in one of his books, seems to have dealt with the problem very wisely, very reverently, in a way to make men pause and take heed to their ways and to walk softly in the presence of sin as awful mystery and the yet deeper mystery of a redeeming Lord "made sin for us that we might be made the righteousness of God in Him." God bless you, dear brother, affectionately.

Often, states Elizabeth, during the last days when he could no longer leave the house for Sunday service, her father would worship with Cadman, sitting close to the radio, ear cupped. And often when a listener asked a question, Brengle would chuckle when Cadman remarked: "I'll do the best I can but I do wish my old friend Commissioner Brengle were here to answer that."

Recognizing forces of evil, a personified spiritual adversary, Brengle yet rejoiced, for he believed it was possible to overcome in this life, indeed to know "heaven on earth." He wanted this experience for all, especially urging it upon his beloved young comrades "in the war," and often counseled fondly but persistently:

My dear Earl, why no note? No victory to record? No text to cheer me? I hope you are all well with victory on your banners and jubilance in your hearts. I've been confined to the house for a week with a heavy cold, but Hallelujah! all is well.

When Earl reported spiritual vacillation and a sense of defeat he urged:

When are you going to close in with God and get it, dear boy? You must put it before everything else and seek with all your heart and God will surely sanctify you. Have a half or all-night of prayer alone, if needs be, but have the blessing. Go for it! Pray through! It may not be easy, but it is the pearl of greatest price, and invaluable things are not gotten easily. You must sacrifice for them and put forth your full strength to obtain them. On God's side it is easy. He waits and longs to sanctify you. But you do not

give Him the opportunity. You pray, but quit just before you have reached
the point where He can do the work in you. You run off to a meal or slip off
to bed, and the Master is left standing there, unable to give you the
blessing.

Get alone with Him now and say to Him as Jacob did at the brook
Jabbok, "I will not let thee go, except Thou bless me," Gen. 32:26. You have
to come to that point some time or never get the blessing. Do it now. Take
your Bible and *Helps to Holiness*, if you think that would help you, and get
down alone with God, and have the battle out. The devil will fight you;
unbelief will assert itself but God is for you. Christ has died. All Heaven is
on your side, while you fight against unbelief and the devil. 'Have faith in
God.' Plead His promises, remembering that He is pledged by an oath to
fulfil them. Hebrews 6:14 to 19.

To support his urging, he would testify:

. . . drifted along just as you have for several years, but at last I had to
settle it one way or the other. I had to fight it out, and I set myself
resolutely to it. Day and night I prayed. I stirred myself up. I didn't want to.
I got indifferent so far as my feelings were concerned, but I forced myself
to pray. I struggled. I cried to God. I listened. I faced my past and confessed
all. I got to the bottom of myself and 40 years ago this coming Friday
morning, January 9, 1885, at about 9 o'clock all alone the work was done.
Hallelujah!

Old age had met Brengle now face to face, and he was neither
surprised nor displeased. It was a curiosity but not a challenge to
Him. He had not dwelt on it in youth, and he did not as he came
close to the great Crossing Over. He regarded it as another gift
from and for his God. He had no fears, no complaints. However, in
later years he spoke more of it as a fact. In October of 1930, he
wrote: "Your good letter received. A man of 30. It hardly seems
possible that it is so long since you began to travel with me! I
wonder if the years fly as fast with you as they do with me. I hardly
think so."

Immediately after retirement he wrote: "Well, they took plenty
of time to get me retired, but I began all over again yesterday, by

preaching at the Christian Alliance Tabernacle, and I have engagements running up into the fall of 1933. It is a joke that I am
retiring." On the general subject of retirement he commented,
"Why this idea of carrying along a lot of retired folk? It may become
a burden to our finance in this period of depression. However, I am
going to live as long as the Lord will let me and try to make it
worthwhile to The Army."

His expressions regarding old age and death increased in the last
days and sometimes he recorded his thoughts in short notes,
perhaps with the view to using them in public addresses, and
sometimes he put such in letters to Earl. A collection of notes were
forwarded to Earl by Elizabeth after his death. The following is
typical:

Many books are written for the young, but I know of but few for old
people. Paul had a very suggestive and divinely wise exhortation for aged
men and women, and David and Isaiah have given us some precious
promises for old people, but generally, old age is not a subject that has
inspired men to write. This may be due to the fact that a man must have
the experience of old age in order to grasp the problems and understand its
trials, its temptations, and special needs, but by the time he has had the
experience his faculties have become chilled by the frost of many winters
and he has no inspiration to write.

But since the harshness of the winter of life has not yet overtaken me, I
shall try to meet the need of some words of comfort, of guidance, of
warning for those, who if not old, soon will be, for old age has needs and
dangers as well as serene peace and compensations. The outward man
perishes, grays, but the inward man is renewed day by day. I am not what I
used to be in many respects, but I didn't use to be what I am today. Earlier, I
was not as serenely assured as I am today. My fears are not so many. I have
proved God and feel that my foundation has grounded and strengthened.

He noted that in old age, moral risks abound, its duties must not
be shirked, its joys needed to be consciously discerned and its
warfare was apparent. "We must go on," he said, "fighting the good
fight of faith for a better world."

As always, he cautioned against a fretful spirit and anxiety for the future:

If God allows me to occupy my body, will He not see that I have food to feed it, and garments to clothe it? He said He would. Matthew 6:25–34. And shall I not trust Him and laugh at fear and be glad? By His grace I will. Nothing is more likely to disjoin our relations with God and precipitate trouble upon us than this faithless anxiety about the future of ourselves and our loved ones. Job said, "I feared a fear, and it came upon me" (Job 3:25).

> Who feareth hath forsaken
> The heavenly Father's side;
> What He hath undertaken
> He surely will provide.
>
> The very birds reprove thee
> With all their happy song;
> The very flowers teach thee
> That fretting is a wrong.
>
> Cheer up! The sparrow chirpeth,
> The Father feedeth me:
> Think how much more He careth,
> O lonely child, for thee.
>
> Fear not, the flowers whisper,
> Since thus He has arranged,
> The buttercup and daisy,
> How canst thou be afraid?
>
> —Anon

Another time he wrote with exuberance of the old-age experience:

My mouth is full of laughter and my heart is full of joy. I feel so sorry for folks who don't like to grow old, and who are trying all the time to hide the fact that they are. I revel in my years. They enrich me. If God should say to me, "I will let you begin over again, and you may have your youth back," I should say, "O dear Lord, if you don't mind, I prefer to go on growing old!"

I would not exchange the peace of mind, the abiding rest of soul, the measure of wisdom I have gained from the sweet and the bitter and the perplexing experiences of life for all the bright but uncertain hopes and tumultuous joys of youth. . . . One of the prayers of my heart, as I grow older, is that of David: "Now, also, when I am old and gray-headed, O God, forsake me not until *I have showed* Thy strength unto this generation and Thy power to everyone that is to come!"

Regarding old age, some lessons that I have learned or partially learned, I here pass on:

1. *Have faith in God:* in His providence, in His superintending care, in His unfailing love.
2. *Accept the bitter with the sweet:* rejoice in both. The bitter may be better than the sweet. Don't grow impatient and fretful.
3. *Keep a heart full of love toward everybody:* If you can't love some with complacency, then love them with compassionate pity, but love them and pray for them.
4. *Don't waste time and fritter away faith by living in the past.* Commit it to God, the bad with the good, and go on.
5. *Give good heed to failing bodily strength:* The Founder (William Booth) once said that the body and soul, being very near neighbors, have a great influence upon each other. We must remember that our bodies are to be treated like our beast, and Solomon says that "a righteous man regardeth the life of his beast."

"As the years march on, In Thee, O Lord, do I put my trust!"

Victory over death was always implied in Brengle's living and preaching. Concerning Earl's ill mother he wrote: "My dear Earl: I am sorry your mother is so poorly, but she must cheer up! Some of her best days may be ahead, and then at the end, *Heaven, Heaven, Heaven* awaits her!"

Two of Brengle's oft used illustrations emphasized his belief concerning death and resurrection. The first, with the Bible reference II Corinthians 5:1, he told of one of inventor Faraday's workmen who clumsily dropped a valued silver cup into a steaming chemical brew. The cup dissolved. Faraday came in, was told and said nothing, but he cast in another acid. The silver precipitated and was sent to Faraday's silversmith and made into a more beautiful cup. "So our bodies," stated Brengle, "will be fashioned like unto His glorious body."

The second, referring to I Corinthians 15:54, described a little girl finding a bird's nest with four speckled eggs. After an absence of some days, she ran to see what had happened and found only broken shells.

"Oh, the beautiful eggs are all spoiled and broken!" she sobbed.

"No, they are not spoiled. The best part of them has taken wings and flown away," said her brother.

"So in death," was Brengle's belief, "the broken shell of the body is left behind, but the spirit has flown away. Hallelujah!"

After a serious illness he wrote: "I shall probably see you and Janet at the General's meetings in New York. What I want to do is to finish well. I haven't many more years and I want to fill them with useful service. See Psalm 71:18."

Gradually, the Brenglian pace was slowing. Gradually he was readying himself for the final great appointment. During one trying illness Janet sent him a poem, which he acknowledged thus:

That was a lovely little poem you sent me. Only it sounded a bit as though you thought I might be going to Heaven soon. Maybe I am, but I'm hoping to live for years yet. But I only ask, "Thy will be done." I want to die at the right time and glorify my Lord in death as in life. We had a glorious Bible class last night. Hallelujah! See John 11:40; 15:11.

Just before his 75th birthday he became very ill. He wrote Earl of the experience:

My eyes are very bad. I cannot see to read. I can write a little, but I write only just when it is necessary. My heart bothers me some too. I had an attack day before yesterday that put me in bed, but not nearly so bad as one I had in fall. I have to exercise constant care, though everybody speaks of how exceedingly well I look. If it wasn't for my old heart, my stomach, my eyes, and my ears, I would be a very well man. Well, Hallelujah! "The outward man perishes, but the inward man is renewed day by day, and I rejoice in my Saviour!" See I Corinthians 15:57, 58.

The condition of his eyes worsened. He wrote of them as of old friends:

. . . My eyes, which have been able to read the finest print through all the years, and which I have used on trains, autos, and in dimly lighted rooms and halls without the least trouble, have suddenly failed me, and I can neither read nor write except in a large, bold hand. Words fade out before my eyes, and the letters get all tangled and twisted. The specialist says I will not be totally blind, and that my eyes will last as long as I do, but if I ever see again to read it will only be after prolonged and complete rest.

This is a distinct loss to me. I can't read my Bible or my songbook, but I am going on by the grace of God, to seek a way to get gain out of loss, and light out of the partial darkness. Quaint old Samuel Rutherford of Scotland, who was greatly persecuted 100 years ago, and in prison for Jesus' sake said that when they thrust him out of God's house and throne room, into the cellar, he always looked for God's wine and he found it. Hallelujah! And he has shared it with the whole church of God. That's what I want to do. Moses got water out of the flinty rock. Samson got honey out of the carcass of the lion which he slew on the way to Gaza to visit his sweetheart. After David's discovery that his little town of Ziglag had been burned to ashes, and his wives and cattle and everything that belonged to his men and himself had been carried away in his absence, he rallied his men, chased the enemy, overthrew them with great slaughter and gathered such an abundance of spoils that he had far more than he had before, and had gifts to give to his friends. That's what I want to do.

Paul got immeasurable blessing out of that troublesome thorn that bothered him and he has shared his blessing with the whole church of God for two thousand years. This affliction gives me new and poignant meaning to the words of Jesus: "The night cometh when no man can work." But then the eternal stars shine out, and then the morning cometh, and the vision of His dear face who loves me, and redeemed me with His own blood, and washed me from my sins and made me a child of the Heavenly Father, so I'm not worrying or murmuring one bit. Remember me in your prayers, and God bless and bless you, dear Earl.

In a letter written in a very large hand near the end, he wrote to Elizabeth:

Darling Ducky, tomorrow I am to come home. It's lovely here (St. Petersburg, Florida) but I'm hungry for you. . . . I feel a bit like a man in prison with my partial deafness and blindness, a bird in a cage. I want to do things and can't. I want to write articles and can't. At least not satisfactorily. But it is all a part of life—and I have wanted to see life whole. So I do not murmur. And "he also serves who only stands and waits," wrote blind John Milton. So I stand and wait. I look up and am glad. My life behind me does not wholly put me to shame, but I wish that from my youth up I had watched, prayed and given myself more wholeheartedly to Him and His service.

In a letter soon after, his spirit seemed to soar higher than ever: "Well, Brother Mallory about every morning says, 'The Lord God omnipotent reigneth!' He cheers his heart with that blessed assurance, and I pass it on to you, Ducky, to cheer your sweet heart."

To an old friend he wrote:

I have sweet fellowship at times in my own room. The saints of all the ages congregate there. Moses is present, and gives his testimony and declares that the eternal God is his refuge, and underneath are the everlasting arms. Joshua arises and declares: "As for me and my house, we will serve the Lord." Samuel and David, my dear friends, Isaiah, Jeremiah, and Daniel, Paul and John and James, and deeply humbled and beloved Peter, each testify to the abounding grace of God. Luther and Wesley and the Founder (William Booth) and Finney, and Spurgeon and Moody, and an unnumbered multitude all testify. Blind old Fanny Crosby cries out, "Blessed assurance, Jesus is mine! Oh what a foretaste of glory divine!" so you see I am not alone. Indeed, I can gather these saints together for a jubilant prayer and praise meeting almost any hour of the day or night, hallelujah forever, and glory to God in the highest!

Three months before his death he acknowledged receipt of one of Janet's poems:

My dear Janet, you have written me a lovely little poem. They are dear little verses; the last one is a note of triumph for which I thank the Lord. Jesus is the Way, dear Janet, and the way He trod is *not lonely.* The Angel of the Lord encampeth round about you and there are unnumbered comrades that are with you in spirit, but Jesus trod the winepress alone and of the people there were none with Him, because He was made sin for us and must bear our cross, the cross, the Heavenly Father's face was hid until he cried out, "My God, my God, why hast Thou forsaken me?" He endured it all that you and I might *never* utter that forsaken cry.

Within the month of his promotion to Glory, the old Commissioner wrote little Jinkie a letter concluding with a passage which applies to his readers today: "From your loving old Grandpa. Here is a text for you: Psalm 100, verse 2: *'Serve the Lord with gladness!'* "

On May 20, 1936, Samuel Logan Brengle was promoted to Glory. George wrote the Army's General:

He seemed well and vigorous in mind and spirit. Monday was a particularly happy day for him. He drove around town shopping with Maude [George's wife] and had a hilarious time at lunch with the children and drove down to meet me at the station at night. After dinner that night he had a bad heart attack, although I don't believe he thought much of it at first. But the little stimulation pellets that he carried around didn't affect it, as they had in the past. I finally helped him into bed, and then got the doctor. The doctor gave him a hypodermic of morphine to ease the pain, which by that time was very severe. The doctor told me that was all that could be done . . . it all occurred just as had been predicted some years ago—the attacks gradually increasing in intensity and ending in a thrombosis.

Browning, in The Primrose of the Rock, speaks of "the faith that elevates the just before and when they die, and makes each heart a separate heaven, a court for Diety." I have seen that faith in operation. Father slipped into unconsciousness sometime after eleven o'clock Monday night. It was hard for him to breathe and the pain was very severe, but right up to his last conscious moment he quoted Scripture and said, "Hallelujah!" and "Praise the Lord!" I was in and out of the room and missed much of what he said, but I can still see the smile on his face as he said, "The angel of the Lord encampeth round about them that fear Him."

While I was out phoning to Elizabeth he quoted the third and fourth lines of the first stanza of Houseman's great hymn: "To Thou that from Thy mansion, through time and place to roam, doth send abroad Thy children, and then doth call them home." The last line has been running through my mind ever since. The earliest times I can remember are of

Father going to and fro on the earth doing good and then coming home to get rested and strength for more work. I am quite sure that for him his death was the last and best and infinitely the most joyous of all his homecomings. May 19, the day before he died—was his and little mother's wedding anniversary, and I think of them now as on an endless honeymoon in that land that is fairer than day. General Higgins (retired) gave Elizabeth father's last letter to him, after reading part of it at the service in the temple. It included :

> My eyes are dim and getting dimmer.
> But on I go and see the King in His beauty,
> And the Land that is far off,
> And yet not far off.

Elizabeth remembers of the Home-going: "Just as his spirit departed on a soft little sigh, a smile came over his face and I believed then, and have ever since, that into that sunlit room, Jesus had appeared to him, and possibly little Mother, and his own mother."

Soon after, Elizabeth in her grief wrote an old family friend, Colonel Blanche Cox, asking, "Oh, why, why couldn't God have seen fit to open our eyes for just a moment and let us see Heaven, too? Catch, if you please, a glimpse through the crack in the door?"

The answer came:

Elizabeth, I firmly believe that the other world is so beautiful and so wonderful beyond our power of thought that if God gave us even a glimpse, we would be useless down here. We would never again be content to live out our lives and do the work on earth to which we are assigned. But truly, the portals of death are garlanded with the flowers of immortality.

Years later, attempting to explain death and immortality to her own son Logan, Elizabeth wrote:

I remember a few days after Grandpa went, I walked out to the old farmhouse down toward the barns and meadows. It was the end of a beautiful day and the sun was beginning to slant. The air seemed completely clear and empty when suddenly the whole air was filled with beautiful shimmering insects. A slight turn of my head and they were gone from sight, another slight turn and there they were again. I was comforted. Perhaps, I thought, living entities can be around us and not seen, perhaps our loved ones too are just as close at times, but our eyes can't catch sight.

About two years before mother died, we moved from Amenia to White Plains. She and Father went down first, and George and I followed the next day. I had never seen the house before, but as we drove up, Mother opened the door on the porch, and smilingly welcomed us in. Instantly, this strange house, in completely new surroundings and typifying an entirely new life was *home*. Mother was there with the same love-lit smile, and that was all that was needed. A whimsy touched me at that instant, though I never dreamed for a moment that she would not be with us for many years; but I thought: "Some day it will be this way in Heaven. Mother will be there a little ahead of us, but when George and I come to the door she will be there with her old, welcoming smile, and all will be well as it is now. And Father will be standing at her shoulder.

In a tribute to his father, George wrote later:

After Father was promoted to Glory, a friend sent us what was perhaps the last letter he ever wrote. In it he told briefly of his increasing infirmity and how his sight was failing. But he said he was discovering the truth of the Bible promise that "at eventide there shall be light"—the inner light that shines for those who are pure in heart and see God. He closed by saying, "So I shout hallelujah! and go on!" These are the words that the family had carved on the stone beneath which he sleeps beside his beloved Lily in the Army corps at the Kensico Cemetery, near New York City: "I shout Hallelujah! and go on!"

Hallelujah! had been Samuel Logan Brengle's watchword. *Holiness* had been his motto. *Amen,* his signet. He helped build the Heavenly Kingdom on earth because he lived in that Kingdom and eagerly invited others to join him. Sam Brengle, like his Lord, made the way winsome and plain.

And a multitude walked there.

A poem found in his writings tells lucidly of his life, his love, and his influence:

Behind, a presence did move,
And grab me by the hair;
And a voice in mastery asked,
                as I strove,
'Guess now who holds thee.'
'Death,' I said, and there
The silver answer rang out,
'Not Death but Love.'

—Anon

APPENDIX

In March of 1935, one year before his death, Brengle was asked to answer questions regarding the hereafter raised by an inquirer of Captain Mary Mason, commanding officer of Morris Run, Pa. Here is his answer:

My dear Mrs. Martin:

Captain Mason has written me stating that you had asked her where souls go immediately following death, whether to a temporary or final resting place.

First, there is a difference of opinion on the part of Christians as to whether the soul of a Christian goes to a permanent place or to a temporary one at death. You know that some believe that most souls go directly to purgatory and are retained there for a definite time, but through various prayers and rituals the soul can be delivered from purgatory rather promptly. Salvationists discard that teaching, the clearest I know being that of Jesus when He said to the thief on the cross, "This day shalt thou be with Me in Paradise," and also when He spoke of Dives being in hell (Luke 16:19-31), and that word of Paul in II Corinthians 5:8 in which it seems He teaches that to be absent from the body is to be present with the Lord and the soul thus present with the Lord is ever to be present with Him. He will never any more lose the presence of his Lord and that Presence will make his Heaven whether or not

Paradise be only a restingplace or the final Heaven to which he is to go.

Personally, I do not consider it profitable to speculate on questions of that character. Moses said in Deuteronomy 29:29: "The secret things belong unto the Lord our God, but those things which are revealed belong unto us and to our children forever that we may do all the words of this law."

I think I have in these passages of Scripture given you about.all that is revealed concerning the immediate restingplace of our Christian dead and of the spirits of the lost, and we simply puzzle our own brain needlessly and unprofitably to be trying to pry any further into the matter. This is enough for our guidance in holy living, which is our chief concern here.

Sincerely yours, in our blessed Lord

In January of 1935, Brengle replied to a serious pessimistic inquiry from a talented young Captain who years later became an impressive officer evangelist. The burden of the inquiry was concerned with evil, revival, and reform. Here are excerpts from the answer:

You write: "I feel the peril of the world is very terrible and that judgment is near, with the Second Coming imminent." The fact is, my dear Captain, the peril of the world has always been very terrible and judgment is always near, but as to the Second Coming being imminent, I am not certain and I would frankly urge you not to be too certain about that. . . . Mind, I do not say that Christ is not coming and that very soon, but do not be carried away with those who are all the time studying the signs. Personally, I feel it very probable that there are mightier revivals to come upon us than the world has yet ever known.

. . . I am a pessimistic optimist. There is so much evil in the world and at the present time it seems to be so largely in the ascendant that I cannot yield to an easy optimism, but on the other hand, there are so many people at this very hour who are crying for the coming of the Kingdom, for the manifestation of God's gracious presence and power and the salvation of men, and there is the love of the everlasting Father, the pitying yearning love and eternal intercession of the risen and enthroned Saviour and the searching and wise ministry of the very present Holy Spirit, that I cannot yield to an easy pessimism . . . nor do I expect Jesus to come in His personal presence and do what He expects to be done through members of His body which constitutes the church. If I might interpret Scripture, when He comes it will be to final judgment, and all that is done for the saving of the world will be done through His people in the power of his unseen spiritual presence and under the guidance and inspiration of the Holy Spirit.

You say you came into The Army to be "a reformer and a revivalist." If God led you in for that purpose, give Him time to prepare you to reform things wisely and to fit you for a revival ministry in our ranks.

Preparation

I never felt that God had brought me in The Army to be a reformer, but I felt that from the very beginning that He had brought me in to be a revivalist and especially on holiness lines; however, it was ten years before I got into that work and those ten years were years of very necessary preparation for the kind of work God wanted me to do.

You say that you had at one time hoped that you might carry on my work when I was gone. I would rejoice to know that this is God's purpose for you. But if it is, like myself, you will have to pass through a period of preparation, of trial, of inward discipline of your patience, your hope, your steadfastness and love, to fit you for it. . . .

. . . I used to feel that I might have a larger field of liberty if I had gotten outside The Army, but it is not the river that just overflows all its banks that does the great work; it is the river that is confined that carries the commerce of nations and that which seems to be cramping you may be that which is necessary to enable you to carry on the most effective work. It is not free steam that drives the engine—it is the steam that is confined in small compass. It is not the powder in the open that explodes and sends its missile afar—it is the powder shut up in the gun barrel. Now, it may be that God wants you to be a soldier or an Envoy, but I do beg of you not to be in haste to resign. I can say to you as Mordecai did to Esther that it may be that God has brought you into The Army for such a time as this.

On Revival

You can have a revival any time. You can begin right now to be a revivalist. Every time you lead a soul into a more simple and daring faith, every time you brighten the hope of a soul and kindle a more burning love and passion for the Saviour, for the glory of God and for the salvation of men, and for a life hid with Christ in God, *you have started a revival*. You can do that along the wayside, anywhere, everywhere. God is ready to revive His work, to refresh His people and we need not wait. We can begin now and where we are, provided there is a revival in our own souls.

On Reform

But reform is different. Institutions and men become fixed. They harden like cement and to reform them is often a very difficult and slow process and you will probably find it so in The Army. To begin with, you are only a young man and a subordinate officer and it will be difficult for you, a youngster, to reform a lot of oldsters. They are conservative. They are part of the system. Their minds are no longer flexible. It is not only so of The Army. It is so everywhere.

Joseph, when only a boy, felt he was to be a leader and he complained of the immorality and evil of his brethren, but he only got himself into trouble, and God had to send him away and to permit the Egyptians to "hurt his feet with fetters," to sorely discipline him. He was laid in iron" we read (Psalm 105) "until the time that his word came . . . the word of the Lord tried him." And after some 13 years of this trial, his opportunity came to mold and fashion his brethren. Moses began as a young man. He was so eager to reform things that he slew an Egyptian and then he had to go to the backside of the desert for 40 years. But his hour came and he wrought mighty deliverances.

Now, don't think you have to run off to the desert. There may be a desert right where you are . . . you will have to be patient, and kindle the same passion that is in your own heart in the hearts of other young men. Don't be a fault-finder. Don't be a kicker. Respect the old men. Pray for them. They have done a brave work and they will soon pass on and then you young men will come to your own and maybe by that time you can effect some reforms.

. . . How Paul wanted to be free and go about evangelizing the world and building up his church, but it was his imprisonments that liberated him to the whole church for all future time, for it was in prison that he wrote his letters. If he could have visited his churches he would not have written these letters. God's ways are not our ways. Be sure that you don't get out of His ways by seeking a greater freedom than you now have. Bide God's time. "He that believeth shall not make haste."

On Reform Methodology

I shall never forget the first time I saw a Colonel with all the mighty breastworks of braid on his uniform. I think it was away back in 1905 or 06 that the uniform was first so decorated. A Chief Secretary, for the first time, came out in this marvelous uniform. I shall never forget how helpless he stood and looked at the audience when the prayer meeting began. He clasped his hands and unclasped his hands, and I looked at him and wanted to both laugh and cry. He looked so pitifully helpless behind those breastworks.

I thought to myself, if that is what we are coming to, the British Empire is safe. London can never be touched. All we have to do is set up a lot of these superior Salvation Army officers with these breastworks and no enemy will be able to get through to attack London. I was myself a Colonel, but I made up my mind that I would never array myself after that fashion. In a continental country, the territorial commander and a Major came to meet me when I landed. They had some business that led them to walk on ahead of my companion and myself and I said to him, "That is a new Major." He asked me how I knew. I said, "Look! His coat is three inches longer than the T.C.'s."

Later in New York, I think about 1909, we had a great congress. I was asked to give a spiritual address on a subject of grave importance. I prepared my head and heart for this address and we had our headquarters filled with officers. General Higgins, then the Foreign Secretary, was present as was our present General (Bramwell Booth). I don't know what led up to it, but I think I was telling about the humility and simplicity that accompanied the highest spirituality, that it led us to be simple in our habits, in the furnishing of our homes and in our clothes. Then I told about this braid on the uniforms and the length of this Major's coat and so forth, much to the merriment of the officers. I said I could tell these new Majors how they could save money—if they would make their coats about three inches longer they could do away with their trousers, but if they would make the waist of their trousers a few inches higher they could do away with their coats. Higgins and the Commander (Evangeline Booth) nearly fell off their seats laughing. There was a perfect riot, and I had some difficulty in getting back to the spiritual purpose of my message, but it started a reform and today we never see a long-tail coat on any officer of any rank in this country.

Excuse me for telling you all this nonsense, but it is not altogether so. It shows how some reforms can be accomplished, not by head-on attack, by lamentations and malediction, but by laughter. It was thus that Cervantes, through his book *Don Quixote,* laughed the foolish and tinseled chivalry of Europe off the stage. It was in this way that Erasmus helped Luther poke fun at pretention. It was so that the prophets of Israel often put the idolatrous and wicked people to shame, and even Jesus, I think, turned the laugh again and again upon the Pharisees. Think of the keen humor and satire in His words: "They strain at a gnat and swallow a camel."

. . . I don't think that by head-on attack you will accomplish anything, but I do believe that praying much, speaking to your immediate superiors and dealing in a kindly way with young people that you can . . . Dear Captain, let us be hopeful, let us not be looking for some great, horrible tribulation to fall upon us, but let us rather look for some great manifestation of mercy and of God's saving power such as the world has not known. May you, yourself, dear Captain, help to bring this about. Have faith in God! "All things are possible to him that believeth."

Eight

The Peaceful Heart

Our introduction referred to a key that can give not only strength to cope with life but also spiritual victory resulting in righteousness, inner peace, and joy. It was this key with which Sam and Lily Brengle unlocked a felicitous life. It was this key that they recognized as the magnet and dynamic of the pioneer Salvation Army. Because of it they joined the organization and because of it they remained in it, despite almost every conceivable provocation and hindrance. Possessing it they marched from this land to the next—singing.

In his preaching and writing, Brengle never described the key experience emotionally, nor did he believe that it came in this manner to most spiritual explorers. He never discredited revelations visited with deep feeling; he knew such himself, but he believed the coveted experience is not one of continual mountaintop ecstasy and is as viable on plateau as in valley. His belief required no "speaking in tongues," emphasis on faith healing, feats of masochistic self-flagellation or denial; no compulsive self-exposure; no accusation or condemnation. It did not demand choice of one religious denomination or school of thought to the exclusion of others; it did not require a formula for church attendance and participation, or for secular pursuit.

The key Brengle lived and taught was, in essence, the lodestar of all religions that recognize and accept the living God as Creator, Saviour, Preserver, and personal Guide for mankind. As apprehended by mankind at the dawn of history, during the historical presence of Christ Jesus, and in this epoch of the etheric Spirit of God, it has been variously designated, "holiness," "sanctification," "baptism in (and by) the Holy Spirit," "the higher-up religion," "the second blessing," "the blessing of a clean heart" and "full salvation." Because of the multiplicity of names and connotations, some of them negatively understood, we propose to introduce one more: *THE PEACEFUL HEART.* Through the years, personal choice and experience have presented many fringe benefits. We do not criticize nor disallow these but seek to describe the key experience as concretely and economically as possible, believing that for each earnest explorer God will create not only "the clean heart" His Scripture promises, but will also add skeleton and flesh of His choosing.

"Peace I leave with you, my peace I give unto you," said Jesus when, leaving this life, He promised the key experience to His followers. *"Not as the world gives, give I unto you . . . Ye shall know that I am in my Father, and you in me, and I in you. . . ."*
—St. John 14:27, 20

The key experience—a peaceful heart—has a single initial requisite: *desire for God.*

Pre-requisite for mature spiritual desire is, of course, the experience of examining the self, admitting inadequacy and willful wrong, including commission of acts that separate from God, making a decision to give one's life to God, and in knowledge of God's sacrifice to justify the unrighteous, accept Christ Jesus and all He represents personally and universally as Saviour and Lord— the loving, accepting, and guiding personal presence of God in history and now in Spirit. This is the treasure chest in which the key rests.

DESIRE: If this already is apparent, we are fortunate; if not, we may conclude it can be activated by natural methods. If malnutrition is caused wholly or in part by lack of appetite, many intrigues are employed to tempt that appetite, including a variety of small doses of food. Appetite is increased by eating. Brengle once prayed, "Oh, Lord, please help me to want what I want to want!" Thirst is often more demanding, though it may well be created and/or intensified by eating salt. "You [Christians] are the salt of the earth," said Jesus. "If the salt has lost its savor, wherewith shall it [the earth] be salted?" That is a singular illustration of the worth of Christians. They are bait, enticement, compelling force when they are "savory" (good to taste).

A DUAL EXPERIENCE? That the forgiveness-peace experience may come in a dual manner is possible and has many times been attested to. That this is not usually the case is so. Natural perception by some persons and understanding of the psyche through personal and/or formal psychological and psychiatric study gives an excellent insight into the need for and possibility of the key experience as the assurance of inner health. And although psychological terminology was not known when The Salvation Army was begun, essential human experience does not change. The change is in man's way of describing it. Brengle often said the initial experience might be likened to falling in love and engagement; the second experience to marriage. A pioneer Salvation Army description suggests that "salvation" connotes the rescue of a drowning man from the storm-whipped ocean of life; he is pulled out of the water into a lifeboat of God's love, often assisted by fellow humans. "Sanctification," (the key experience) is likened to the rescued man receiving resuscitation—the waters of contamination being squeezed out of him. General Frederick L. Coutts likens the "saved" man to a beginning brass-band aspirant, given a horn, a tune book and the attention of a teacher; the "sanctified" man as one accepted into the band under the leadership of a conductor who not only knows the difficult score but, hearing every note played, often corrects individual players so that the music may be as mellifluous as the Composer intended.

Of some people, contemporary thought demands the recognition that inferior, negative and/or harmful personal action is of secondary importance spiritually; primary evil lies in man's intention—his will. Civil law may confuse attention to clear thinking here. Necessarily, it judges overt action first, intention second; but spiritual law *always* reverses the two. Though Scripture is explicit, much religious thought, especially during the Victorian era of the 1800s, has more often dealt with act than intention, concerning itself almost exclusively with externals.

If self-intention is early recognized, the experience may be entire though growth will necessarily begin at that point as, naturally, all life either grows or atrophies. Also, revelation increases as desire and commitment intensify. If converted very early, some children may never consider manifestation primary, especially if they have not committed gross acts; however, many adults come to God in crisis need—loss, self-indulgence, self-denial: they seek forgiveness, comfort, and guidance—all geared to self need. The key experience then is sought some time later, when a man realizes that spiritual maturity means something more than forgiveness for manifest sins. At this point, many explorers have an intense yearning for a "higher up" experience, one that they soon recognize has quite other goals than self-satisfaction, and they begin to seek not a blessing but the Blesser, desiring to give God not only first place but also owner occupancy, and to dedicate the self to help build His Kingdom of love "on earth as it is in Heaven."

The fact that preaching, teaching, and testifying regarding the key experience had never been popular, did not deter Brengle who concurred with William and Catherine Booth that preaching it often meant trouble. He once wrote: "Do not think you can make holiness (the key experience) popular. It cannot be done. There is no such thing as holiness separate from Christ in you, and it is an impossibility to make Christ Jesus *popular* in this world. . . . Do not waste your time trying to fix up a popular holiness. Just be holy because the Lord God is holy."

The pioneer Salvation Army also proclaimed that acceptance of the key experience committed a person to concern about and care for others. Bramwell Booth stated: "In no department of its teaching has The Salvation Army suffered more reproach than in this: "HOLINESS UNTO THE LORD." Indeed, its teaching, as distinct from its methods, has, apart from this, been largely welcomed by every section of the professing Church . . . it has aroused opposition, not merely from the intellectual apologist for existing systems, but from the thousands whose half-hearted service and unwilling consecration it has condemned.

"Because the holiness (key experience) that we contend for is a fighting holiness, a suffering holiness, a soul-saving holiness; in short, Jesus Christ's holiness. Any mere enjoyment of religion or 'waiting on God,' for 'fullness of blessing,' which has not immediately and indissolubly joined with it the instant rescue of sinners from their sins, is in our judgment a mere caricature of the higher life of communion with Christ, which the word of God declares to be the highest of all."

Definition of the Key Experience: A Peaceful Heart

The following presentation is based on the writings and letters of Samuel Logan and Elizabeth Swift Brengle, the doctrine book of The Salvation Army and personal thought, prayer, and commitment. Let's begin by listing what the peaceful heart is *NOT:*

1. IT IS NOT ABSOLUTE PERFECTION: the perfection which

belongs to God only and which never can be increased or diminished. Jesus referred to this when He said: "There is none good but one, that is God."

2. IT IS NOT ADAMIC PERFECTION (sometimes called sinless perfection): or the perfection of innocence enjoyed by Adam at creation, when he could perfectly obey God's law. We are rendered imperfect both in mind and body and God does not expect the impossible.

3. IT IS NOT INFALLIBILITY: or freedom from mistakes in judgment. This would require perfect knowledge, which none of us has. It does, however, help us in judging, through reliance on God's Spirit.

4. IT IS NOT FREEDOM FROM BODILY OR MENTAL INFIRMITIES: many earnest godly people have been great sufferers; it does, however, require the dedication of suffering to God, often implementing faith which does affect gradual or swift recovery. A knowledge of and acceptance of the mind's role in governing the body supports this contention.

5. IT IS NOT FREEDOM FROM TEMPTATION: Jesus, although without sin was "sorely tempted," and the first couple were tempted when holy. Often the more advanced a man becomes in his spiritual life, the more fiercely "the powers of darkness" attack him, especially mentally. The key experience does bring victory over temptation.

6. IT IS NOT A STATE OF GRACE FROM WHICH IT IS IMPOSSIBLE TO FALL. All spiritual attainment rests upon consciously and continually living up to spiritual light.

7. IT IS NOT A STATE WHEREIN FURTHER ADVANCE IS IMPOSSIBLE: All spiritual attainment rests upon the natural principle of growth.

Now, we'll consider what the peaceful heart *IS:*

It is the self freed of self will, put under the complete control of

God. It is the soul captured and captivated by Divinity, who is apprehended as personal and all-loving; the soul eager only to do and be what glorifies God, characterized by creative love that has for its object, God. The overflow of such lives is the "living water" that helps cleanse and sustain other lives and appears to encompass all nature, *not only human life*. It denotes the true conservation approach to life—cherishing all life because all life is of God. It not only lives but must help live.

The peaceful heart becomes such when God as Spirit is perceived as Personal and allowed to become the great Friend-Controller in the most intimate manner. Listening for God's direction and following it is all-important, but it is imperative here to note that God's voice of revelation will *NEVER* oppose the recorded ordinances of God (the Holy Scriptures). The Voice may be tested by business-like conversation with God, demanding persistence and specificity, and never discounting man's responsibility for thought and industry. God at no time does man's work. He empowers and invigorates for that work, and sometimes speeds the working of His laws when man reaches an intensified point of faith. But God begins miraculously when man gives all he is capable of. No matter how great your talent, He won't practice your violin for you, and He will seldom even purchase it.

Brengle said of the Holy Spirit in men's lives:

When Jesus came, a body was prepared for Him and through the body He wrought wondrous works; but when the other Comforter comes, He takes possession of those bodies that are freely presented to Him, and He touches their lives with grace; He shines peacefully and gloriously on their faces. He flashes beams of pity and compassion and heavenly affection from their eyes; He kindles a fire of love in their hearts, and lights the flame of truth in their minds. They become His temple, and their hearts are a holy of holies in which His blessed Presence abides. From that central citadel He works, enduing the man who has received Him with *power*. . . .

Now, what fire and electricity and magnetism do in iron and steel the Holy Spirit does in the spirits of men who believe on Jesus, follow Him wholly and trust Him intelligently. He dwells in them and inspires them, till they are all alive with the very life of God . . . they will have power over the world, over the flesh and over the devil.

Bramwell Booth spoke of the indwelling Christ as "our helper":

In the work of righteousness He is a partner with us. In the life of faith and prayer He is our unwavering Prompter and Guide. In the submission of our wills to God and the chastening of our Spirit, He is the great co-worker with us. In the bearing of burdens and the enduring of trials and sorrow He joins hands with us to lead us on.

Another time Brengle attempted to define the key experience thus:

Do you want to know what holiness is? It is pure *LOVE*. Do you want to know what the baptism of the Holy Spirit is? It is a baptism of love that brings every thought into captivity to the Lord Jesus, that casts out all fear, that burns up doubt and unbelief as fire burns trash, that makes one "meek and lowly in heart," that makes one hate uncleanness, lying, and deceit, a flattering tongue and every evil way with a perfect hatred that makes Heaven and hell eternal realities, that makes one patient and gentle with the froward and sinful, that makes one "pure . . . peaceable . . . easy to be entreated, full of mercy and good fruits without partiality, and without hypocrisy," that brings one into perfect and unbroken sympathy with the Lord Jesus Christ in His toil and travail to bring a lost and rebel world back to God.

Now we'll consider specific instructions.

How To Have a Peaceful Heart:

1. DESIRE: born of conviction of the inadequacy of self. Often, as described previously, evil intentions, unrecognized and confronted, trouble explorers after "salvation," such as pride, vanity, selfish ambition, evil temper, malice, covetousness, lust, sloth, undue possessiveness, envy and dishonesty. They may be either manifest or unmanifest. This desire is not for an experience which

will make people self-proclaimed martyrs. Brengle called these the "misery hunters." "They are seeking something hard to do. It is not joy they want but misery . . . they are good and do good. But what they need is a faith that sanctifies." Also, those err who seek happiness instead of holiness. Happiness is a by-product and is often confused with self-indulgence and self-gratification. The secret of life is not self-actualization or the desperate current urge to find, satisfy, and please self but to "actualize" God—to find, satisfy, and please God! *"I AM THEIR REWARD,"* He says of earnest seekers.

2. RENUNCIATION: this is the second condition for a peaceful heart; that is, giving up everything that is known to be opposed to the will of God. This includes habits of thought as well as of speech and deed.

3. CONSECRATION: this is the third condition for a peaceful heart; that is, the dedication to God of the self and all its posses-sions, to live only to please Him and do His will. Renunciation and consecration differ from each other in that renunciation means giving up what is *against* God. Consecration means giving all to be used *for* God.

4. FAITH: that is, the simple heart trust that God accepts the self and will control it completely and purposefully in love, accord-ing to His promise. The realization of God's acceptance sometimes evokes an emotional response; however, this is not generally so. What is termed "assurance," does follow, with or without deep feeling, often some time later. Assurance means a deep sense of settlement, of peace and purpose and acceptance by God—and an increasing sense of love for all of life.

Brengle repeatedly avowed that there are two kinds of faith: the *GRACE* of faith is that which is given to every man to work with, and by which he can come to God. The *GIFT* of faith is that which is bestowed by the Holy Spirit, when a man has exercised his faith to its utmost. The searching faith means a man will say, "I believe God will bless me," and goes forward in the light he has. At some later point, often suddenly, God breaks through with added assurance and gives a sense of certitude that *all is well*—often using some Scripture portion, testimony, inward reasoning or other device. Now the explorer can say, "I *know* in whom I have believed. God is blessing me right now!" Childlike faith has come as a Divine gift; the seeker takes hold of the promises of God—and clings without burden or pressure. When you *know* you do not fret. You trust.

There are marvelous results of the key experience. Here are some:

Results of the Key Experience:

1. INWARD PEACE—the natural outcome of all controversy with God having ceased.

2. A GREAT SENSE OF JOY USUALLY. When assurance came to Brengle two mornings after his consecration had been made and the initial experience accepted, he reported: "I got out of bed and was reading some of the words of Jesus, HE GAVE ME SUCH A BLESSING as I never dreamed a man could have this side of Heaven. It was a heaven of love that came into my heart. I walked out over Boston Commons before breakfast weeping for joy and praising the Lord. Oh, how I loved! In that hour I knew Jesus and I loved Him till it seemed my heart would break with love. I loved the sparrows. I loved the dogs. I loved the horses, I loved the little urchins on the streets. I loved the strangers who hurried past me. I loved the heathen. I loved the whole world. . . ."

3. A SIMPLE, CONSTANT TRUST IN GOD: everything and everyone matters a great deal but nothing matters too much.

4. A PERFECT AND HEARTY AGREEMENT WITH THE WILL OF GOD: to go anywhere, do anything without resistance.

5. LOVE TO GOD AND MAN: expressing tenderness and

alertness regarding others. Selfishness goes when love comes. Of this, Brengle said: "If we ask for success, it is not that we may be exalted, but that God may be glorified, that Jesus may secure the purchase of His blood, that men may be saved, and the Kingdom of Heaven be established upon earth. If we ask for daily bread, it is not that we may be full, but that we may be fitted for daily duty. If we ask for health, it is not alone that we may be free from pain and filled with physical comfort, but that we may be faithful in fulfilling the work for which God has placed us here."

6. PROGRESS IN SPIRITUAL LIFE AND INCREASE IN USE-FULNESS: a holy life is attractive. If example is more powerful than precept, a pure example must be more effective than an impure one. A peaceful heart brings quiet power. Striking and remarkable things will begin to occur. It will become increasingly generous with time, attention, and money.

Brengle noted this in his own behavior:

. . . since then I have found it easier to give than to withhold. I began by giving one-tenth of my income, but I could not stop there. Any case of need, any appeal for help wrung my heart with an anguish of desire to give, until if it were not for the foresight of a prudent wife, who gets me to lay up money with her for a needed suit, I should frequently be without suitable clothes to wear. This is not natural—it is spiritual—supernatural. In the old days when I had plenty of money, I can remember that it was rather grudgingly that I subscribed two dollars a year to the support of the Gospel. I should be decidedly ashamed to tell this, but for the fact that I am now "a new creature" and honest confession is good for the soul. Instead of finding my feet on quicksands, I found them on granite, and instead of starvation, I found plenty. There is a Divine philosophy in self-denial that the wise folks of this world never dream of!

The key experience also changes a person's attitude regarding his own importance and rights. He is secure, at peace—in God. He no longer needs to argue every point to a conclusion. He no longer has to defend himself or berate himself. He does not argue. "Remember, if you want to retain a clean heart," stated Commissioner Dowdle, one of the Army's pioneer "pile drivers," "don't *argue!"*

Brengle was asked if others will not then "walk over us if we do not stand up for our rights?" His answer was classic:

I do not argue that you are not to stand up for your rights, but that you are to *stand up for your higher rather than your lower rights,* the rights of your heavenly life rather than your earthly life, in the way and spirit of Jesus. If men wrong you intentionally, they wrong themselves far worse. And if you have the spirit of Jesus in your heart you will pity them more than you pity yourself.

One of his favorite stories concerned a corps officer who discovered that his predecessor was writing back to corps folk for money. He became incensed and reported the action, and the *coat* was returned ("if he ask your coat give him your cloak also"). The *coat* was returned but nothing good came of the incident, and the officer "got lean in his soul." He had quenched the Spirit of God. He had broken the law of the Kingdom. Not only had he refused to give his cloak but also he had fought for and secured the return of the coat. Brengle admonished and advised that he should have felt, "Poor fellow. He must be hard up. I will send him five dollars myself. He has taken my coat. He shall have my cloak also." When this was explained, said Brengle, "He came to himself very quickly and was back in the narrow way rejoicing."

7. DEVOTION TO THE SERVICE OF GOD.

8. READINESS TO WITNESS FOR CHRIST JESUS AND TO THE KEY EXPERIENCE. Shyness will gradually slip away, and a spontaneous naturalness supplant it.

9. COMPLETE VICTORY OVER ALL IN THE SELF THAT IS PERCEIVED TO BE UNLIKE GOD—thus, a perfect will because it is given entirely to God.

Now, to the care of a peaceful heart. Enjoying the key experience the explorer will become more sensitive to self and to others and will not despair when falling or failing. He is human and may at times unintentionally blunder and hurt. When this happens, he will feel intense pain but will immediately confess to God, be forgiven and proceed, making restitution when possible. One difference between an earnest and an insincere person is that the former will agonize over self-failure or hurt to others and immediately attempt to make right. The self-directed person will care little and not seek to correct.

Maintaining a Peaceful Heart Requires:

1. PRAYER: This means more than devotions. In addition, there will be a definite period set aside daily for conversation with God in a natural, unselfconscious manner regarding all that concerns life. Prayer, to be most effective, should be specific (generalized questions bring generalized answers), expectant, earnest, and positive. You've got to mean business. Of this Brengle wrote: "The secret of all failure, and of all true success, is hidden in the attitude of the soul in its private walk with God. The man who courageously waits on God is bound to succeed. He cannot fail. Jesus puts the secret into these words: 'But you, when you pray, enter into your closet and when you have shut your door, pray to your Father which is in secret. And your Father which sees in secret shall reward you openly.' Matthew 6:6. All failure has its beginning in the closet, in neglecting to wait on God until filled with wisdom, clothed with power, and all on fire with love."

William Booth once stated in an officers' council: "Remember to take time to pray God's blessing down on your own soul every day. If you do not, you will lose God. I am a very busy man, but I take time to get alone with God every day and commune with Him. If I did not, He would soon leave me."

The Brengles set aside an hour a day as a minimum. Sound impossible? All talent and skill must be developed, practiced. Superior proficiency comes with superior practice. *THERE IS NO*

OTHER WAY. How strange that we demand a 20 minute sermon yet spend three or four hours a day indiscriminately before a winking and sometimes hoodwinking television set.

2. BIBLE READING: the Bible should be treated as the great treasure chest of man. Delight and curiosity will increase as he studies, and soon it will not seem study at all but adventure. Reading should be daily, regular, and should be done with the purpose of knowledge and wisdom but most of all for inspiration. Like the "talking books," for today's children, it will speak when opened.

Brengle marked his Bible continually, almost haphazardly—marked and marked and marked; quoted and quoted and quoted. He recommended this practice to others and also recommended that officers always read a portion when they visited, marking a chosen Scripture for those they visited. Such a practice, he proved, often brings unexpected rewards. Of such he recounted: "Many years ago in Nashua, N.H., I asked permission of a lady in whose home I was being entertained, to mark a text in her Bible. Years later we met and she reminded me of it, saying, 'An infidel came to our home after you left and was railing against God and religion. My Bible was lying open on the table. He took it up, and his eyes fell on that marked text. It smote his heart and conscience. He fell under deep conviction and was converted as a result of the reading.'"

Many translations and versions are now available at modest cost. You may choose from the most scholarly Greek-English versions to the most simple modern language paperbacks. If you are uncertain or do not have the price of a Bible, write me.

3. PRACTICING THE PRESENCE OF GOD: He is now acknowledged to be within you. Watch, listen for Him. Enjoy His presence. Brengle conversed with Him as with a beloved Friend. So may we.

4. LIVING EXPECTANTLY: be done with all negativism. Life

will become a marvelous adventure, and you may watch with ease as God works out his pattern and purpose in your life. Remember, He cannot make a mistake—if you trust.

5. PRAISING GOD: In thought, speech, and deed express thanksgiving—no matter what. This is one of the great secrets of victorious, powerful living—there in *every* circumstance is the seed of victory if in "all things" we give thanks, not just *in* but also *for,* no matter how unlikely the circumstance. Praise, Brengle believed, is a pleasant and safe substitute for fault-finding and slander: "Be filled with the Spirit; speaking to yourselves in Psalms and hymns and songs, singing and making melody in your heart to the Lord; *giving thanks always for all things unto God."* Eph. 5:18.

He wrote often of praise: "We have a right to rejoice, and we ought to do it. It is our highest privilege and our most solemn duty. And if we do it not, I think it must fill the angels with confusion and the fiends in the bottomless pit with a kind of hideous joy. We ought to do it for this is almost the only thing we do on earth that we shall not cease to do in Heaven. Weeping and fasting and watching and praying and self-denying and cross-bearing and conflict with hell will cease. But praise to God, *hallelujahs,* shall continue eternally."

Lily Brengle found her greatest spiritual difficulty when, totally given up to God but encountering great mental turmoil when many burdens befell, she was almost overcome. She had not sinned nor resisted the Spirit, but a failure to rejoice in Him had in a measure quenched the Spirit. She had not turned on the main, and so her soul was not flooded with living waters. Then she remembered the command: "Thou shalt rejoice before the Lord thy God in all that thou puttest thine hands unto!" Deut. 12:8, 18.

REJOICE!

WE SHOULD PRAISE GOD TO OTHERS FOR OUR PEACE-FUL HEART: talking about a peaceful heart may at first seem formidable, even impossible. Lily Brengle knew this temptation and guided many others regarding it:

> After the Christian has been sanctified by God's Spirit, usually the first temptation which comes is to conceal the fact. This temptation is so usual, so subtle in its approaches, and so fatal when yielded to, that it is a chief weapon against the soul. One reason for such a testimony is that this glorifies God.
>
> "I want to live it and not talk about it," says the poor Christian, harassed by thoughts that people will call him conceited, spiritually proud, blasphemous. But if you succeeded in living the life of perfect love without professing it, the people about you would inevitably ascribe much of the merit to you. And God states: "My glory will I not give to another."
>
> Another reason for testifying (to a peaceful heart) is that such encourages others. A comrade recently wrote me: "No one ever yet got the blessing from simply seeing someone else live it. The testimony must always go with the life to make it effective." If I am cured of a terrible cancer, it will do no good (in helping others) for me to go around living my good health. I must tell you who cured me and how, if I would honor my physician and do good to other sufferers. "Ring out the good news all over the world! If a man will be holy, he must give God all the glory. And if he does he must 'Tell how great things God has done for him!'"

SHOUTING: A final comment regarding praise emphasizes a kind of expression encouraged in early Army days but not popular now—it is shouting. In a somewhat sedate society where intelligence and good manners restrain spontaneous expression—except at sports events—it may seem incongruous to many readers that shouting is recommended, even advised by such as William Booth and Samuel Brengle, but such is the case. Catherine, Booth's eldest daughter, stated: "Nothing fills all hell with dismay like a reckless, dare-devil shouting faith. Nothing can stand before a man with a genuine shout in his soul!" Shouting, Brengle believed, is the "final and highest expression of faith made perfect in its various stages. Where there is victory, there is shouting, and where there is no shouting, faith and patience are either in retreat, or are engaged in conflict." There is a Scriptural seal of approval on the *Amens!* and *Hallelujahs!* and *Praise the Lord!:* "And then the Lord Himself shall descend from Heaven with a shout, with the voice of the archangel and with the trumpet of God" and seeming defeat shall be turned into eternal victory!" I Thess. 4:16.

6. REALIZING STEWARDSHIP: A peaceful heart makes people responsible, dependable, eager, and self-confident because reliance is in God with whom all is not only possible but purposeful, practical, and praiseworthy.

7. CHOOSING THE BEST: Quality persons make quality selections and the possessor of a peaceful heart, being made worthy, acceptable and loving, considers every detail of life important. All is of God and meant to glorify Him. He will not settle for mediocrity but ever strives to present himself and all that concerns him *a living sacrifice* to God. This necessitates strict discipline of self, a growing sense of selectivity, and the awareness of quality. He will find himself increasingly doing better than his best, because in his eagerness and aspiration he is complemented, extended, and ornamented by God.

As with all in nature, there are always active opponents to a peaceful heart. Let's consider the most obvious:

Hindrances To Keeping a Peaceful Heart:

1. TEMPTATION: Temptations will assail as always, but the explorer may be victorious if he trusts completely and *substitutes* something worthwhile for them. Focusing attention on them, praying against them, has the worst psychological effect and only intensifies the temptations. Recently, a woman of high intelligence, realizing that smoking harms the lungs, smoked two packs of cigarettes as she begged God to remove her desire for them!

Sometimes, unusual temptations, especially mental ones, come to the truly dedicated person. Brengle noted of this kind:

You remember that it was after Jesus was baptized by the Holy Spirit that he was led into the wilderness to be tempted of the devil for 40 days and 40 nights. Your trials and temptations will lead you into a deeper acquaintance with Jesus, for as He was so are you to be in this present world. Remember, he said, *"My grace is sufficient for you."*

Temptations regarding feeling often torment. Brengle knew such a person who for several days said she felt nothing. Then the thought came to her that no doubt God was working as He promised despite her lack of feeling, for she had met the conditions; and that she must just act as though the deed was done. As she counted it accomplished, assurance came and a sense of peace with it.

Especially when an explorer has known exaltation he tends to be tempted to despondence when he is not excited. Brengle observed,

Do not think, however, when the tide flows out to low water mark that the Comforter has left you. I remember well how, after I had received the Spirit of the Lord, I walked for weeks under a weight of divine joy and glory that was almost too much for my body to bear. Then the joy began to subside, and there would be alternate days of joy and peace. And on the days when there was no special experience, the devil would tempt me with the thought that I had in some way grieved God and that He was leaving me. But God taught me that I must "hold fast the profession of my faith without wavering." So I may say to you, do not think He has left you because you are not overflowing with emotion. Hold fast your faith. He is with you and will not leave you. The Holy Spirit is not capricious and fickle.

2. SEARCHING UNNECESSARILY: Many people get into confusion after the initial acceptance and when feeling runs low, believe they are forsaken and begin begging for His return. This is foolish, wasteful, and enormously fatiguing, dulling the self and creating a state of anxiety, which certainly does not glorify God. Seeking Him as though He had not already come:

If you will seek light when you have light, you will find darkness and confusion. Have faith. Scripture testifies: "Therefore, having received Him into your hearts, continually acknowledge His presence, obey Him, glory in Him, and He will abide with you forever." St. John 14:16. Do not keep seeking and crying for more power, but rather seek by prayer and watchfulness and study and the honest improvement of every opportunity to be a perfectly free channel for the power of the Holy Spirit—*who is now in you.*

3. ALLOWING FATIGUE TO OVERWHELM: The body is the temple of the living God and must be treated with sanity and care. Do not become overtired if possible or you will be taunted with a sense of exaggeration of difficulty and distress.

4. ALLOWING TOO LITTLE TIME FOR GOD: We live in His presence, but without meditation upon Him, praise to Him, and time to listen quietly for His directions and assurance of love, the experience will be hindered. Put God, and the practice of His Presence, *first.*

A peaceful heart may be forfeited altogether. Then what? Fortunate we are if we realize the tragedy soon. But no matter what, we must set ourselves to regain it.

Losing a Peaceful Heart:

Perhaps the greatest number of people lose the key experience because it is not what they expected. Said one woman to Brengle: "I have given up all, but I have not the happiness I expected." To which he responded, "Ah, the promise is not unto them that seek *happiness* but to them 'which hunger and thirst after *righteousness.* They shall be filled.' Seek righteousness, not happiness."

The difficulty of this loss is in the person's self and not in God, according to Brengle:

It is difficult for us to trust one whom we have wronged, and the difficulty is doubled when that one has been a tender, loving friend. Many people fail at this point by constantly looking for the same emotions and joy they had when they were first saved, and they refuse to believe because they do not find it. Do you remember that the children of Israel went into captivity several times after they had entered Canaan? But never did God divide Jordan for them again. God never took them in again in the same manner as at first. God says: "I will bring the blind by a way that they know not. I will lead them in paths that they have not known." You cannot walk by sight. You *must* yield yourself to the Holy Spirit and He will surely lead you into the promised land. Seek simply to be right with God.

John Wesley stated that he believed people usually lose the blessing several times before they learn the secret of keeping it. You prove your real desire and purpose to be holy, not by giving up in the presence of defeat, but by rising from ten thousand falls, and going at it again with renewed faith and consecration. The promise is: *"SEEK AND YE SHALL FIND."* How long keep seeking? Till you find. Suppose you lose it? Then seek again. God will surprise you some day by pouring out such a full baptism of His Spirit on you that all your darkness and doubts and uncertainty will vanish forever, and you will never fall again, and God's smile will be no more withdrawn, and you will never more go down. You must seek for hidden treasure then diligently cherish it.

Finally, be ready to accept chastisement, for it is one of your greatest means of growth. Brengle delighted to use a personal illustration when discussing the Scripture portion, "Those whom I love I chasten." He told that when as a boy he was naughty and had to be punished, "Mother could never understand why I kept so near to her when she took the long cane to whack me. But you see, the nearer I got to her, within her arms, the lighter fell the strokes."

This, then, is an outline of the way of the key, *a peaceful heart.* It is offered in the belief that God's Holy Spirit is today urging us to seek Him. Some of us are antipathetical to religiosity, to sacrament and symbol, to temple and tabernacle. We do not want a present but a Presence. This is God's voice calling in our yearning. If you are among these spiritual explorers, we invite you to seek a peaceful heart. Meeting the necessary conditions, and praying, "God, cleanse me from all unrighteousness and create in me a clean and peaceful heart," it shall be done. Count on God. *He has no alternative* and must keep His promise both to forgive and to cleanse us from all unrighteousness. Count on God.

Should you desire to ask questions, receive counsel or materials, please write. Know that you are, as a reader of this book, prayed for daily and that a new life of peace, purpose, and victory awaits you.

May we share an illustration from the earliest days of The Salvation Army as our parting salute? It's the story of Charlie, an illiterate factory worker, who came tumbling out of a saloon into an open-air ring, where a meeting was being conducted by 19-year-old Bramwell Booth. Charlie knelt at the drumhead, unable to resist the message of Jesus. Faith in a risen Saviour who cared even for "the likes" of him made Charlie ecstatic. He gave himself completely to God and was determined to testify. Bramwell dissuaded him because of a striking impediment in his speech. He stuttered uncontrollably.

"A bit later," Bramwell promised, hoping to protect him from the raillery of his old drinking pals. But Charlie persisted. Finally, he was permitted to speak. As Bramwell had anticipated, out staggered the good old boys, throwing bottles and stones, cursing Charlie. But he testified for more than five minutes. Finally, they tired and stood silently listening as Charlie, bloodied and beaten, extolled a love that made him glow. Many pals followed him to the Army hall that night and succeeding nights.

A few months later, Charlie reported, "Mr. Booth, everybody at my lodging house has got saved."

"Well," said Bramwell, "smiling and half-facetious, "then, Charlie, I think you'd better change lodging houses every two or three months." Which Charlie did—until two years later when, mortally injured in a factory accident, he called for his young friend, and Bramwell hurried to his side. Charlie said he wanted to sing a farewell song as he went marching through the Golden Gates, and Bramwell joined him:

> Then in a nobler, thweeter thong,
> I'll thing Hith power to thave;
> When thith poor lithping, thammering tongue
> Lieth thilent in the grave. Hallelujah!

That's what a peaceful heart is all about.

Will you, beloved reader, accept the key to victory?

Appendix

General Frederick L. Coutts (R) on Brengle as a writer:

Brengle wrote to meet the need of the hour. "Write a book about holiness for young people," said Bramwell Booth, and *The Way of Holiness*, published in 1927, was the result. Several years earlier the Army in the United States had been shaken by a top level crisis, and Brengle had been shaken with it. He had written a series of papers—later published as *The Soul Winner's Secret*, and of these a leading officer said, "Your writing probably did more to turn the minds of our people from self to souls . . . than did any other person or agency."

Because he wrote to meet a need, Brengle, like the Apostle, put much of himself into his writing. Students have worked over the Pauline letters to deduce the nature of the Apostle's own spiritual experience, and any Salvationist student in search of a thesis could set about combing the pages of Brengle's eight books in order to reconstruct his personal beliefs, for though much that he wrote was unrelated in the sense that it first appeared as disconnected newspaper articles, yet sentence is knit to sentence and page to page by the common bond of the writer's experimental knowledge of the sanctifying power of God.

"I have put into them," said Brengle of the 28 chapters which make up *Resurrection Life and Power*, "much of my own experience." This would be true of most that he wrote. Like Bunyan, he preached what he 'smartingly did feel.'

. . . Brengle [his writing] defies the touch of time and, having sold by the million, still sells. He must have what it takes. First, he has the human touch. Perhaps his secret is that he wrote from his heart to the needs of the human heart. This does not mean that he said the last word on the doctrine of holiness, or that the figures of speech which he employed to make visible and tangible an inward and invisible spiritual experience are as sacrosanct as the tables of stone. But it does mean that he seized upon certain imperishable aspects of this doctrine which lifted his writing from the timely to the timeless.

A second secret is that Brengle saw that the doctrine of holiness is not the enemy of the heart's affections but their sanctifier. In a world where sex has become an obsession—the spice of fiction and the sauce of the film, as if forbidden fruit is tasty only because it is forbidden—Brengle deserves a monument for his acceptance of men and women as God made them. To quote:

"All the appetites and desires of the body are normally perfectly innocent. The sexual desire is no more sinful normally than the desire for food and drink. None of these desires is destroyed by the grace of God, but they are brought under subjection to the law of Christ. . . . Their appeal is instinctive, and the first instinctive movement is not under the subjection of the will. But immediately the intelligence takes cognizance of the instinctive movement, and the appeal is presented to the will for a decision for or against. At that point the sanctified soul must assert its loyalty to the law of Christ." Here is neither denial nor license but the law of Christian liberty.

A third secret is that Brengle found the key to the experience of holiness in the word *Christlikeness*. There are many names for the experience of holiness. Our doctrine book lists more than a dozen. Each can be supported by texts—sometimes from the Old Testament, more happily from the New. *But no one is saved by a name.* We can choose our names, for example, between "a clean heart" and "the second blessing." Various people have had various preferences. According to his biographer, General Bramwell Booth set great store by "perfect love." Begbie has written of the Founder's references to "the higher up religion." Commissioner Watmore held that this experience meant "a life lived in harmony with the known will of God." Brengle found the thread through the yarns which some have darned by words without knowledge in the truth, that the same "Christ in you" who is the hope of glory, is also our hope of holiness.

There is no higher holiness than growth in Christlikeness. This tree, like every other, is known by its fruits. Holiness is a character judgment. It may or may not be accompanied by varying degrees of emotionalism. The entry into the experience may be visible to all present or known to God alone. A man may be fulsome or reticent in his testimony but his actions will speak. For whatever pious phrases a man may employ, only that life is holy which is Christlike.

The life which is not Christlike, whatever religious garb it may wear, is not holy. A life of abstention is not of necessity a life of holiness. The life of holiness is pressed down, shaken together and running over with those outgoing qualities of light and love which marked the manhood of the Master. Holiness is the highest expression of that life more abundant of which Jesus is the Giver. There can be no conflict between the work of the Holy Spirit and the example of Jesus. The work of the Divine Agent is to make us like the Divine Son.

National Brengle Institute

Concerning the National Brengle Institute which has met annually since 1947, Colonel Albert Pepper, first principal, recounts:

On August 4, 1947, 42 delegates from all parts of the United States met at the Salvation Army camp, Camp Lake, Wisconsin, for the first session—a two-week session. We felt that we had reached the ultimate, but each successive year has seen the institute grow in depth, in usefulness and in influence.

The institute stems from a suggestion made in 1946 by General Albert Orsborn, who was on a visit to the United States. He thought that it might be an excellent plan to establish a Brengle College where "scriptural holiness would be taught and retaught." Commissioner Norman S. Marshall, the Central Territorial Commander, offered the use of the school for officers' training in Chicago and services of the staff to initiate the program. Because I was the principal I was named dean of the institute. The Brengle staff, composed of experienced men and women, bear the burden of planning and thought for the institute throughout the year, remembering the basic purpose of the institute:

1. To exalt the Lord Jesus as an uttermost Saviour from sin and to unfold the glorious meaning of holiness.

2. To inspire the officer-student to enjoy in his own heart a personal experience of entire sanctification and to endorse the experience by voice and life.

3. To imbue officers with a sense of personal accountability to spread the gospel and to lead people to victory in Christ.

Brengle Remembered

The following are excerpts from a provocative article by Commissioner Francis Evans:

I once heard Brengle use this illustration in a meeting. "'How can we be assured of the divinity of Christ?' you ask. A man born blind may hear a thousand testimonies to the beauties of the starry heavens and the glories of sunrise and sunset, and yet doubt it all. Is there any way to destroy his doubts forever? Only one, and that is to *give him his sight*. Then he will doubt no more. He knows. He sees for himself."

The Bible was his handbook. He never preached anything he did not find in the Bible. He was also a great Bible student, varying his methods, using now synthesis, now analysis, or spending time on Bible doctrines, Bible characters etc. People asked:

> "What is the secret of power?"
>   "Waiting on God."
> "What is the difference between consecration and
>   sanctification?"
>   "The first is giving to God; the second, receiving from God."
> "How shall I know that I am accepted of God?"
>   "There is but one way, and that is by the witness of the
>   Holy Spirit."
> "Why should we be holy?"
>   "In order that we may be made useful."
> "How may I keep the blessing of holiness?"
>   "You must be quick to obey God."

He was a specialist on holiness. He devoted his time and studies mainly to the study and teaching of the doctrine of holiness as taught by Wesley. For that reason he is probably a better guide than some of his theological critics. Certainly he "talked about God," and that is theology!

Bibliography

Begbie, Harold. *The Life of General William Booth*. New York, McMillan and Co., 1926.

Benton, Itzhak. *Stalking the Wild Pendulum*. New York, E. P. Dutton Co., 1977.

Booth, Bramwell. *Echoes and Memories*, New York, George H. Doran Co., 1925.

_____. *Papers on Life and Religion*. The Salvation Army, 1920.

_____. *Servants of All*. London, The Salvation Army, 1914.

_____. *These Fifty Years*. London, Cassell & Co. Ltd., 1929.

Booth, Catherine. *Papers on Godliness*. London, The Salvation Army, 1881.

_____. *Popular Christianity*. London, The Salvation Army.

Booth, William. *Religion for Every Day*. London, The Salvation Army.

_____. *Salvation Soldiery*. London, The Salvation Army, 1886.

_____. *The General's Letters*. London, The Salvation Army, 1886.

Booth-Tucker, Frederick. *The Life of Mrs. Booth*. London, The Salvation Army, 1893.

Brengle, Elizabeth Swift. *Drum Taps*. London, The Salvation Army, 1886.

————. *Half Hours with My Guide*. London, The Salvation Army, 1914.

————. *What Hinders You?* London, The Salvation Army, 1908.

Brengle, Samuel Logan. *Ancient Prophets*. London, The Salvation Army, 1929.

————. *Heart Talks on Holiness*. London, The Salvation Army, 1949.

————. *Helps to Holiness*. London, The Salvation Army, 1896.

————. *Love Slaves*. London, The Salvation Army, 1923.

————. *Resurrection Life and Power*. The Salvation Army, 1925.

————. *When the Holy Ghost Is Come*. London, The Salvation Army, 1909.

Burnell, Genevieve. *The Golden Thread of Reality*. New York, Hastings House, 1967.

Douglas, Eileen. *Elizabeth Swift Brengle*. London, The Salvation Army, 1922.

————. *Francis the Saint*. London, The Salvation Army, 1927.

Drummond, Henry. *The Greatest Thing in the World*. Kansas City, Hallmark Cards Inc., 1967.

Hall, Clarence W. *Portrait of a Prophet*. Chicago, The Salvation Army, 1933.

Irvine, St. John. *God's Soldier*. London, William Heinemann, Ltd., 1934.

James, William. *The Varieties of Religious Experience*. New York, The New American Library, 1961.

Jones, E. Stanley. *The Divine Yes*. New York & Nashville, Abingdon Press, 1975.

Martin, Malachi. *Jesus Now*. New York, E. P. Dutton & Co., 1973.

Menninger, Karl, M.D. *Whatever Became of Sin?* New York, Hawthorn Books, Inc., 1974.

Mollenkott, Virginia. *Adamant and Stone Chips*. Waco, Texas, Word Inc., 1967.

Read, Edward. *Studies in Sanctification*. Toronto, The Salvation Army, 1975.

Salvation Army, The. *Handbook of Doctrine*. London, The Salvation Army, 1935.

_____. *Holiness Readings*. London, The Salvation Army, 1891.

_____. *Orders and Regulations for Field Officers*. London, The Salvation Army, 1919.

Smith, Hannah Whitall. *The Christian's Secret of a Happy Life*. Westwood, N.J., Fleming H. Revell Co.

Snider, John D. *The Vision Splendid*. Washington, D.C., Review and Herald Pub. Assoc., 1959.

Starcke, Walter. *This Double Thread*. New York, Harper and Row, 1967.